NATIVE
AMERICAN
WOMEN'S
STUDIES

PETER LANG
New York • Washington, D.C./Baltimore • Bern
Frankfurt am Main • Berlin • Brussels • Vienna • Oxford

Stephanie A. Sellers

NATIVE AMERICAN WOMEN'S STUDIES

A PRIMER

PETER LANG
New York • Washington, D.C./Baltimore • Bern
Frankfurt am Main • Berlin • Brussels • Vienna • Oxford

Library of Congress Cataloging-in-Publication Data

Sellers, Stephanie A.
Native American women's studies: a primer / Stephanie A. Sellers.
p. cm.
Includes bibliographical references.
1. Indian women—United States—Social cónditions.
2. Feminism—United States. I. Title.
E59.W8S44   305.48'897—dc22   2007005744
ISBN 978-0-8204-9710-5

Bibliographic information published by **Die Deutsche Nationalbibliothek**.
Die Deutsche Nationalbibliothek lists this publication in the "Deutsche
Nationalbibliografie"; detailed bibliographic data are available
on the Internet at http://dnb.d-nb.de/.

Cover design by Joni Holst

The paper in this book meets the guidelines for permanence and durability
of the Committee on Production Guidelines for Book Longevity
of the Council of Library Resources.

© 2008 Peter Lang Publishing, Inc., New York
29 Broadway, 18th floor, New York, NY 10006
www.peterlang.com

Printed in the United States of America

I dedicate this work to the Native American women of the Americas who spend their lives honoring their cultures by perpetuating them among the rising generations, fighting for rights for their nations and the earth, and educating the world about their traditions and national causes. Your nations and this world are indebted to you.

In particular I wish to honor Barbara Alice Mann.

A nation cannot heal until the dignity of its women is restored.

Contents

Acknowledgments   xi

CHAPTER I.
Introduction and Overview   1

CHAPTER II.
Textbooks, Lectures, and Projects   13

CHAPTER III.
Women's Studies Terminology and Concepts
from a Native Perspective   49

CHAPTER IV.
Native American Terminology for the Women's Studies
Classroom   69

CHAPTER V.
Patriarchy, Colonial History, and the Waves of Feminism   83

CHAPTER VI.
Native American Women Today   107

Works Cited   119

Acknowledgments

I would like to gratefully acknowledge the elder colleagues who helped me by commenting on parts of the manuscript and offering encouragement: Temma Berg and Jean Potuchek of Gettysburg College, and Barbara Alice Mann of the University of Toledo.

I am also grateful to Heidi Burns, senior editor at Peter Lang, who offered important suggestions for revisions and much patient and generous encouragement.

A special thanks goes to Sophie Appel, production supervisor at Peter Lang, for her generosity in formatting the manuscript.

CHAPTER I

Introduction and Overview

This book is for the college classroom as well as nonacademic organizations that serve women and support their empowerment and education, like Survivors, Women in Need, and national organizations such as Coalition Against Domestic Violence, women's shelters, and women's therapy groups. Topics in Native American women's studies are empowering choices for annual women's conferences, workshops, seminars, and retreats. Disseminating information about the cultural legacy of gynocratic Native American nations can work as an insightful tool for broad social change and for increasing Native cultural awareness. Most importantly, it gives voice to the experiences of Native American nations, particularly the most underrepresented voices of all: Native American women.

The Idea for the Course

I began teaching about Native American women in a team-taught "Women of Color" class in 2000. I was responsible for a month-long segment. To my surprise, the multiethnic and multiracial women in the public university class were deeply moved and ultimately changed how they understood themselves as women. They wrote long testimonials about how their lives, sometimes filled with shocking abuse, would be so much different if they had lived in a world still governed by the clan mothers of the Eastern Woodlands. The women students spoke in class and in their reaction papers about enduring all manner of difficulties in their lives solely because of their gender: rejection by religious institutions and family members for getting pregnant before marriage, not feeling safe in the world at large, feeling silenced around their boyfriends or husbands, and so on. Though epiphanies are not uncommon in the women's studies classroom in general, what does stand out in the Native American women's studies classroom is the students' recognition that their experiences are specific to the culture they were born to, and that alternative ways of perceiving women are made available to them for the first time. More than one Native woman came to me after class in distress and said, "So many Natives have forgotten the old ways [that respected women], especially the men."

When the semester ended, I received letters and emails from students declaring that after they learned about the precolonial traditions of Native Americans, they would never put up with abuse again because the Native grandmothers would not want them to do so. They felt quite connected to these ancient grandmothers and to their cultural philosophy. Several students each academic year confided in me that now they could "never go back" to someone or some institution or some former belief about a woman's identity and social status. I also received stony silence and near emotional paralysis from some women, particularly nontraditional-student-aged, married women, who could not so easily make the choice of not returning to a husband or a religious group. I found their situation and conflict particularly poignant. Overall, those first semesters of teaching Native American women's studies materials were academically and emotionally challenging and empowering for me. Time and again I witnessed profound epiphanies in my women students, and I began to understand that I was engaged in an experience that reached far beyond academics.

A few years after the team-taught class, I developed an entire semester-long course titled "Native American Women," which quickly filled to capacity and soon after was offered both semesters each academic year. Male students began to enroll in higher numbers as well as overall course capacity increased to thirty, which is quite high for a small liberal arts college where I now teach. Clearly students are drawn to this class, to this information, and to this experience of personal growth. The quality of student work in my Native women's class exceeds all other classes I teach, and the rich connections I make with my students across the disciplines lasts beyond the semester, even beyond graduation.

So what creates such a response in students? I believe it is simple: the women learn of another model for constructing beliefs about being women, and it redefines women's place in human systems that deeply honors them. There is no such model in western culture, and the women students are starved for meaningful examples of what being a woman means. Right at the beginning of class when students learn of Sky Woman and Spider Woman, they are stopped in their "patriarchal tracks." What occurs is the internalization of valuing women: women's bodily functions, women's psycho-spiritual experiences, women as political leaders, women safely moving in their own community, women as healers, women as the source of all manner of life. Male students also are empowered to see themselves as integral to the nourishment—biological and spiritual—of their community. In other words, students recognize that to Native traditional cultures human beings have profound worth, sacred purposes, and are members of a broad community—and the students recognize that they do also. The course essentially reconfigures students' sense of worth as women and as human beings—from isolated model to a connected one. That experience is emancipating from the modern ideology that edifies rugged individualism, women as victims and sex objects, and men as perpetrators and emotionally detached "machos."

As a woman committed to empowering women and looking for ways to bring healing to western culture's gender-based conflicts, which I see as one of the fundamental causes of all current human social problems, this course is important to me. Last year I took the course out of the privileged academic environment and held a summer-long workshop with the professionals running a women's organization in the town where I live that offers legal advocacy for domestic violence victims and a women's shelter. Most of the women had at least an undergraduate education, but not necessarily any women's studies courses. Some women had no college at all. They were at first stunned to silence to learn about Native women's centrality in their nations; then they were outraged by the prevailing American system that marginalizes women in ways they had not realized before. A common exclamation from the legal advocates was "Ha! No protection-from-abuse orders needed and judges telling our women clients they were to blame for the fight with their male partner that put them in the hospital!"

What these women taught me, and what my students continue to teach me, is that education is power—personal empowerment—and that if to the contrary a woman is taught that her gender is flawed and has been flawed since the beginning of time and she deserves secondhand citizenship status from every corner of her world, she will believe it. This course of study offers women another model for life, and although we cannot, and perhaps do not need to, reenact the clan mothers' system exactly, it is a real and true way women and men lived and made this world on Turtle Island, as Native Americans of the Eastern Woodlands have called and still call this continent. That knowledge is power. Empowered women, and men, can change the world to a more equitable global society. The farther information about women and men in traditional, gynocratic Native cultures is disseminated, the greater our chances as a global nation that we can grow, evolve, and end the gross social inequity from which the majority of the American and world population suffers. What we need to evolve to are the indigenous systems that were far more philosophically advanced and balanced than western culture. Further, it will bring to the fore the issues indigenous women and their nations face today, and the many organizations and strategies they have created to cope with contemporary problems resulting from European colonization—all from a very-much-alive traditional cultural philosophy.

I invite you now to join the growing number of educators in the academy and outside of it to offer teachings about the lives of

Native American women to audiences who are ready to listen. This cultural legacy offers healing for both Native and non-Native women in a world that continues to be fraught with conflict that especially targets women. Herein are some solutions and possibilities for moving forward to wholeness and the healing of humanity and our earth.

Foundational Information in Indigenous Cultures Relevant to the Course

In upcoming chapters and in the textbooks I recommend for the course, there are complete discussions about the cultural practices and theories I note in brief below. What is listed here should serve as a preliminary synopsis of essential Native cultural understandings about life, and the list can also be used as a quick reference tool for both the instructor and students. This primer is meant to be used as a guide, not the source of cultural and historical content for the course; the texts listed in upcoming chapters will provide the necessary cultural information and theoretical perspectives.

First of all, creation stories of Native Americans are nearly all based in multiple creators: females, males, transgenders, and often animals. In many cosmologies women are centrally figured, and some names of these divine beings are Sky Woman, Thought Woman, Corn Woman, Spider Woman, and First Woman. There is seldom a singular, male god as we have in western culture with its three monotheistic religions: Judaism, Christianity, and Islam. Each Native nation has its own creation story, and they vary widely. The cosmologies are important to note because they re-

Third, Native women's roles changed dramatically during colonization because, among other reasons, the colonizers believed in and practiced a patriarchal governing and social structure. This structure was antithetical to Native governments and societies, and therefore the Native system posed a direct threat to the beliefs of western culture that centralized only men. Further, through forced assimilation often enacted through missionary schools, over the past several hundred years some Native people began to reject their own culture that centralized women because they were told it was wrong, even "savage" and "ungodly" to believe in it anymore. Doing so is called "internalized racism": the belief that what racists think about the people they are discriminating against, even hating, that the members of that hated group then adopt the beliefs about themselves and think they are actually true. This type of cultural genocide has pervaded most Native nations, and traditional people today are fighting to keep their traditions alive in the present generation. Though a college course can never take the place of traditional elders teaching the next generation of Native people about their culture, it can help with those efforts especially for the millions of Native people who are disconnected from their community because of former forced assimilation and fleeing from American military threats—only half the population of indigenous North Americans live on a reservation.

Fourth, the terminology used in the classroom or workshop is important. Indigenous peoples name themselves as First Nations, Indigenous Americans, Indigenous People, Native North Americans, Native Americans, Natives, American Indians, and Indians. What I recommend to students is to be consistent and mindful of their choice. The term "Native Americans" can sometimes suggest erasure for South and Central Americans and Canadians since "Americans" most often denotes only citizens of the United States and not of the two other Americas. "Indians" can be offensive to some Native peoples because this is the misnomer of Christopher Columbus who believed he had sailed into India and therefore named the Native people "Indians." Some Native people only use the term "Indian" to name themselves however. The term "First Nations" is a declarative statement about who was here first, important because some anthropologists suggest that indigenous peoples were not originally from the Americas and therefore have no claim to the land. I use the term "Native North Americans" or simply "Natives" because I primarily speak about the cultures of the indigenous peoples living in the continental United States.

Another important consideration in word choice is the use of the term *tribe*. To some Native peoples this is a slur because indigenous peoples have nations, not tribes. Use of the term *tribe*, to some, is an attempt by settlers to debase the complex cultural nations of the indigenous people and render them impotent, cultureless savages. For example, we would never say the United States is a "tribe"; indeed, it is considered a formidable nation, just as most Native nations were vast, formidable nations before the colonizers arrived. The term *tribe* is also a reference to an early anthropological belief that Native Americans were the lost Jewish tribe of Israel: this is utterly false and quite offensive to Native peoples. I encourage students to use the term *nation* or *community* when referring to the social and governing structures of Native peoples today, and discourage use of the western cultural term *tribe*.

Fifth, the origination of humanity and earliest human movement within the Americas held by Native peoples differs from the scientists of western culture. Native peoples have the oral and written records within their nations that demonstrate that their people migrated *from* North America out *to* other continents such as Asia and Europe not the reverse. Native scholars are rightfully offended when they are told by non-Native anthropologists that academia "knows better" than the indigenous nations do about their own people's history. Further, non-Native scientists hold many theories about the land, animals, climate, and events happening in the Americas that Native experts and traditionals utterly discount as false. One example of this misconception is the origination of the horse in North America. Indigenous nations assert that horses have always lived in North America and were not brought by the Spanish as non-Native historians and anthropologists claim. Indeed, recent archaeological evidence and DNA studies on horse fossilized remains demonstrate what indigenous peoples have claimed all along: the horse is from North America. See the Winter 2007, Volume 8, No. 4 edition of *National Museum of the American Indian* journal for an article on this topic.

For further study on the important issues concerning significant discrepancies about archaeological, geological, and historical perceptions that westerners and Native Americans believe about indigenous peoples, I recommend the book *Red Earth, White Lies and the Myth of Scientific Fact* by Vine Deloria, Jr. Therefore, for an instructor of a course studying Native American women, it is essential to validate and acknowledge that these are important differences between Native cultures and western culture and that Native perspectives are legitimate and valid. Remember that discounting the experiences of some people—women and all minorities—as inadmissible in a court of law against an Anglo male was only recently, and certainly still not entirely, eliminated from our judicial system. Unfortunately, the same practice still prevails in the documents supported in academia about indigenous peoples, and scholars need to be aware of this fact when conducting research.

Sixth, all indigenous nations have a relationship with the earth and are communal people. This is a broad, sweeping statement about thousands of nations of people around the world that have widely varying cultures, languages, histories, and myths; however, it is simply true. Relationships with the natural world and communal ethics are primary cultural definitions that set indigenous nations apart from the nations of western culture and of industrialized nations today. How the earth is named, conceptualized, and the multitude of different ceremonies conducted to communicate with or revere her vary widely among Native nations; nevertheless, all Native nations do indeed revere her and see her, literally and metaphorically, as the source of all life. Communal ethics, though expressed and conceptualized differently from nation to nation, is another defining cultural practice of indigenous peoples that is absent in western culture and contemporary industrialized nations. Some Native academics argue that the purpose of academia insisting that Native nations are all radically different in every conceivable way is not to honor them, but to continue to divide them and thus weaken their political power in dealing with encroachments on their rights, sovereignty, and land.

Last, instructors of the course should remind students that the traditions of Native peoples are not a thing of the past but are still part of the living culture of indigenous people today. The people, cultures, languages, and the wisdom of the past are not dead, but are vitally alive in the culturally identified Native American people living in the United States and in every country on this planet. Many still hold their council meetings in their original languages and conduct their sacred ceremonies as they have been conducted for thousands of years.

A course in Native American Women's Studies is part of the ongoing testament of the endurance and survival of indigenous peoples in the Americas and throughout the world. The course should be an experience of empowerment for students who should come to conceptualize women, men, power, and their relationship with the earth in a more connected, holistic way. The legacy of Native Americans is a needed source of wisdom that can help humanity return to a philosophy of wholeness that once successfully governed this land for millennia. Non-Native American peoples can benefit from understanding and practicing traditional indigenous ethics in contemporary institutions (like the classroom, community groups, local politics, and ultimately national leadership), and they can return the benefit of this teaching by standing up for indigenous peoples' struggles for rights.

CHAPTER II
Textbooks, Lectures, and Projects

What must be established at the beginning of a course in Native American Women's Studies is an understanding that western or mainstream American culture and the cultures of Native Americans are fundamentally different. These differences determine how students will understand the notions of power, women, men, and every system constructed by human beings that result from those understandings. The course should address the traditional roles of Native American women from precolonial contact, how they changed during colonization, and the challenges facing Native women (particularly Native women leaders) today. Students will most likely have very little background information about Native American people or culture. Therefore, it can be helpful to them in a 200-level course to offer an opportunity for biographical research on Native women early in the semester, that is presented to the class, in order to offer some general background on the Native nations.

What is primary in the course objectives is to teach students how women are conceptualized as beings functioning in a social system that is based in the cultural beliefs of the culture in which

they have been born and raised. Sexuality, personal empowerment, identity-shaping, opportunities for leadership, and social
expression are all based in cultural beliefs as well. Thus, how
women of western culture are conceptualized is quite different
from how Native women are, and these radically contrasting con-
ceptions alter women's lives, their choices, and their experiences.
A paramount goal is to draw attention to these differences in culture for the purpose of noting that, unlike the belief of western
culture, all women were not submissive, exploited, or the targets
of male violence since "the beginning of time" as ordained in the
religions and social practices of western culture. What transpires
in the classroom among female and male students is an epiphany
that is life-transforming: Non-Native women have no other model
than the patriarchal one in which they were raised to define themselves unless they were deliberately reared in an environment that
actively challenged patriarchal constructions. They have seldom
heard of a matrilineal people and most often believe it is pure
fairy tale. Once the Native precontact models are shown to them, a
change within them (sometimes radical) occurs.

Professors of the course, workshop leaders, and students will
need to engage in "Native American Cultural Awareness" thinking or in what I have dubbed their "Native mind" when discussing the history, social structures, literature, and contemporary
experiences of Native people. Native mind can be developed
through a simple, but profoundly meaningful exercise the first
day of class and be deepened as the course progresses.

Native Mind Exercise

In order to introduce students to the concept of developing their
Native mind, the instructors might bring a tree limb to class. They
will hold up the limb and ask the class, "What is this?" They will
most likely respond with, "It's a twig. It's a stick." Then ask students if this twig or stick has life, spirit, or intelligence. They will
most likely respond with a strong, declarative, "No!" They may
express clear indignation at the thought of, what is to them, an
inanimate object possessing life and spirit. Instructors will then
engage in a Native understanding of the object by noting: "This is
part of a tree. It is connected to the tree. It has life, spirit, and intelligence. It possesses consciousness. It has a memory. It has a relationship with the other beings around it. It is a member of this
community for I have taken it from the ground beneath a tree on
this campus. Perhaps this particular type of tree is a medicinal
one; its bark is possibly used for a healing tea. The tree is quite
old, therefore, it should be referred to not as an 'it' but as Grandmother." Non-Native students will be astonished at these asser-
tions. Indeed, it is the beginning demonstration of the incredible
gulf between the two cultures' understanding of life.

Next, instructors might ask, "What if I held a human finger or
arm before you and asked you what it was?" Students will be a bit
mortified at the thought of this, but will declare, "We would ask,
whose is it?" They would recognize at this point that parts of
some beings (like trees) are perceived in western culture as not
belonging to anything else, even to the source from which they
originate. This perception of parts belonging to a whole only applies to humans, since in western culture humans are perceived as
having the highest value of all beings and, most importantly, liv-

ing objects are perceived as being separate, individual entities not as connected to one another. For example, trees are not perceived as being connected or in relationship with humans, birds, or the earth, except for a merely biological, unconscious connection. In Native cultures, the opposite is true. Trees, birds, algae, and so on, in other words the entire biosphere, are understood to be relational, consciously in connection with one another in a global, interconnected, interdependent, spiritually alive community. In some Native cultures it is understood that every life form has its own spirit song.

A second exercise to cultivate a mindset of Native communal ethics is the following: Ask students to mindfully look across the crowded dining hall of their school at mealtime and say silently to themselves, "These people are all my relatives, my brothers and sisters." This exercise will elicit powerful responses from students. Some comments I have received include: "It was so weird thinking I'm related to people I don't even know," "I actually looked a couple of people right in the eyes when I said the words to myself and I got this rushing feeling—like it was really true," and "It was the first time in three years I ever looked at anyone in the dining hall besides my friends!"

Another request I often make of students is to take time outside of class to stand still and look at the sky or the earth for a timed minute: just quiet observation of earth or sky. Responses are typically the same year after year. They come to class and exclaim, "Wow! I'm twenty years old and it's the first time I think I ever really looked at the sky—really looked at it! Awesome!" When I press them for analysis about how such observations might influence them, they often say, "If you notice something, it starts to matter to you because you can't care about something you never even knew existed or just took for granted." Obviously, this is the course's goal for Native American women's experiences: educating people so they not only notice the women's experiences, but become personally concerned about their relatives' contemporary plight.

What these exercises demonstrate are the Native cultural values of honoring the whole of life, i.e., communal ethics. These principal values will be repeatedly demonstrated throughout the course and are essential requirements to understanding the texts, research projects, and the experiences of Native American women of the past and of today.

First Lectures

Interspersed with first reading assignments should be discussions that expand on the cultural beliefs of most Native nations. Though a "pan-Indianism" cultural approach is inappropriate for any course in Native American studies, noting that there are important, fundamental similarities among indigenous nations is readily observable and are, therefore, legitimate points to note. Some essential cultural points to thoroughly address are:

- western culture's hierarchy of existence model versus the communal ethics model of First Nations peoples;
- the western cultural valuing of singularity and the Eastern Woodlands and many other indigenous nations' worldview of balanced pairs;
- the cultural concept of human power.

By the second week of class these cultural differences, along with the creation stories of a few Native nations, should be discussed via lecture and course readings. The goals of the lectures are to direct students' minds away from western cultural thinking to a Native perspective of existence, and to prepare students to think about women and men in a way that is entirely different from western culture's version. Of course, there are varying perspectives held within western culture and its subcultures, and it is a culture that has changed dramatically over the centuries. However, there are fundamental threads of belief that set the values and worldview of that culture, which is the backbone of mainstream American culture. These values are expressed in the nation's social and political practices. It is these fundamental, widely held and expressed beliefs that I place under the general header of western culture.

It is essential to achieve the teaching goals of centering an indigenous worldview because without these understandings, students will not be able to conceive of the notion and duties of traditional Native women, but will think of them only within the constructions of western culture. In other words, Native women will be perceived as being culturally and historically the same as EuroAmerican women, only wearing feathers and blankets.

On the first day of class I also ask students to write a list of images, words, and beliefs about Native American women that they have learned throughout their lifetime. Then I ask them to note the source of those images and beliefs. After five minutes or so, I instruct them to gather in groups and discuss the list; this discussion is then opened up to the entire class. I ask students to save this list in their notebooks because, unbeknownst to them, at the end of the semester I ask them to get out the list and read what they wrote. They are indeed shocked when they reread their original notions about Native women after a semester of intense study.

Communal Ethics versus Hierarchy of Existence Models

By the second or third class a discussion about differing cultural perceptions of life is necessary. The professor may write on the board a ladder under the heading "Western Cultural Model." She or he may then ask the students, "According to westerners/ EuroAmericans/non-Natives, what is the most important being on the planet?" Students will readily respond with, "Humans," or "we are." The professor then writes "humans" on the first rung of the ladder. A subsequent question is, "What is next? What beings are the second most important ones on our planet?" They will, again, easily recognize that the number two slot on the hierarchy of existence according to westerners is animals. The professor will then write "animals" on the second rung of the ladder. This manner of inquiry should continue until all the levels of existence of our planet are written on the ladder in the following order: trees, plants, insects, rocks, dirt. Students seldom differentiate among animals, birds, or fish and sometimes they say insects have less importance than dirt.

Next, the professor should motivate the class to think deeper about the beings listed on the rungs of the ladder. Are there hierarchies within this larger one? For example, among the first category of "humans," are there hierarchies? Professors may wish to set a few minutes aside for small-group work and have students discuss the subhierarchies of each category contained within the larger one. Some possibilities for responses include the hierarchies of gender, race, and class within the human category. Students may recognize that heterosexual males, people with light skin and hair, and people who are wealthy are understood by the mainstream to be at the top of the subhierarchy of humanity. Domestic animals (like personal pets) are perceived to have more value than wild animals; plants with beautiful flowers have more value than plants that are considered "weeds"; rocks and dirt are considered to be the most valueless things on our planet, and so on. These are some possible responses.

After this exercise, inquire about the reasoning behind the hierarchy. For instance, why are humans considered to be the top or most important being in the hierarchy? Students will say, "Because humans are smartest! Look at all the things we have developed (technology). We can write and think. We have souls." A few students may say, "Humans know there is a god." Then the professor may inquire, "Why are animals at the number two slot; why are they perceived to be the next most valuable creature after humans? Why aren't rocks in the number two slot?" Students will note that animals are somewhat similar to humans: they are mobile, bleed, reproduce, make sounds, and have a life-death cycle. Students will be hesitant about declaring animals to be without a soul. They may believe that wild animals do not have a soul, but their beloved pet at home certainly does, they will argue. They will declare that animals do not have real intelligence, but engage in route behaviors that are learned, not from the result of insight or spiritual knowledge (a few students will tentatively argue with this point, being somewhat timid in front of a dissenting class, however). Pressed for the reasoning behind this thinking, students will not be certain how to explain the conflict in their belief. Next, inquire about trees and plants. Students will now be certain that plants do not have a spirit nor do they communicate with each other or with humans; some students may feel that trees have a soul and intelligence. Last, few, if any, students will say that insects, rocks, or dirt have intelligence, spirit, or much value beyond the basic necessities of their presence in the biosphere. Some science students may point out the roles of these beings in the natural world, but the same students will quickly note that their purposes are to uphold the food chain and that rocks and dirt are not living. This ends the "ladder" portion of the Hierarchy of Existence model present in western culture.

It is important to note to the class at this point that there are certainly individuals and some non-Native groups in the United States who do not align themselves with these beliefs. Even so, this cultural conceptualization of life on our planet is based on the principles and values created by western civilization. These beliefs are espoused in the religious and literary texts of that culture and are expressed by people living in the culture whether they are aware of the texts, practices, and beliefs or not. In other words, whether an individual non-Native American person is intellectually aware of the cultural principles that created western culture and mainstream American culture, that person, just as all students in the classroom, will be able to readily observe their belief that humans have the most worth above all other beings and dirt has the least worth of all. Cultural beliefs are indoctrinated into human beings with their first interactions as infants and toddlers, and they come to be understood as "organic" to them, but they are not. Cultural beliefs and values, of course, are learned. Therefore, non-Native American peoples learn and come to live one type of culture and Native American peoples have another.

One important concept also expressed in the western cultural model that is imperative to recognize and discuss with students is the value of the "I" or of the individual. In western culture the individual is at the number one slot on the ladder. The professor may wish to query students about the books they have read throughout their education, particularly literature in the English department. "Who is written about in these books?" the professor may ask. Students will quickly acknowledge that they are about individuals, primarily and almost solely, men. Themes from these works like the hero, the savior, the adventurer, the conqueror, and the warrior are about pitting one man against other men, nature, or his own internal conflicts. These are fundamental literary components from the English tradition and will be easily recognizable to most students. What they all have in common is the centralization of men and, most importantly for this discussion, the individual human. Coupled with the individual focus is conflict, whether it be external or internal or both. The centralization of the individual is in nearly every literary classic in the western tradition; however, it does not appear in the traditional stories of Native peoples. What is central or "number one" to Native peoples is the "We" of the nation and the biosphere, not the "I" of one human self. Students will see this demonstrated repeatedly in course readings from the creation stories to traditional stories to contemporary stories of Native people.

Next, draw a circle on the board and above it write "Native Communal Ethics." Begin a lecture about the cultural beliefs and values held by Native peoples in relation to all the beings on earth. First and foremost, the professor must emphasize that all beings on our planet, including Mother Earth herself, are considered to be:

- members of the community;
- in relationship with each other;
- intelligent, sentient, conscious, and having spirit;
- able to communicate to human beings if they wish to.

It is most necessary to point out to students that these are not modern, New Age-type notions; hippie thinking; fairy tales; idealization of "Indian" spirituality; indeed, they are not Disney or Hollywood movie material. These notions are also not *Lord of the Rings* or *Harry Potter* fantasies. They are not science fiction or Marvel comics either. The professor must impress upon students that the aforementioned perspectives about the whole of life on our planet are firmly, traditionally, and historically based in Native cultural knowledge and traditions. They are not inventions. The people of the Eastern Woodlands have been saying "Mother Earth" for millennia; the term is not the invention of bumper sticker manufacturers. Although not every Native nation uses the literal term Mother Earth—important to know to avoid generalization of Native cultures—they all certainly do understand their people to be in relationship with her.

Students will inquire with expressions of disbelief, "Plants can talk?!" The appropriate answer is: "Yes. In the Native tradition plants clearly communicate with the people who have been specially trained to communicate with them—and sometimes just with people who can listen properly." The important point to convey to students is that whatever the being is—algae, perch, sand dollar, King Fisher, giant sequoia—that being has value, purpose, and intelligence according to the communal beliefs of Native peoples. What that ultimately means is that every life form on our planet has the right to be considered in the affairs of humanity; they have the right to be treated with respect.

Now, the professor should ask the class while pointing to the circle written on the blackboard, "Where should I write the word human on this circle? Where should I write the words birds, plants, butterflies?" The students will understand that these beings have equal importance to Native peoples and they can be written anywhere on the circle. There is no ladder, no hierarchy, in Native cultural perspective or precolonial practices. Perhaps a student may ask at this point, "What about leadership? Wasn't someone in charge?" This is an excellent question. The answer will unfold in the next lectures and through course reading.

Metaphor of One versus Balanced Pairs

Native American academics, particularly Barbara Alice Mann, have observed that western culture is based on singulars, on "ones." Mann has dubbed this cultural phenomenon as "Metaphor of One" thinking, which she discusses on page 173 of her book *Native Americans, Archaeologists, and the Mounds* (2003). Metaphor of One thinking is expressed in western culture through the adherence to the notion that multiples of anything are illegitimate or suspect, and that there is only one true, legitimate version of anything (173). Some examples of this dynamic are the western cultural belief in one god, one life, one soul, one true love, and one version of the truth (173). The professor might ask students what we say in western culture when our "true love" ends and we find another "true love." Students will quickly say that the first one was not really real, it was false, and the new love is really the true love. Another example teachers might use for illustration purposes is by asking the class, "Which creation story is true? Which one is the real one?" This may be in reference to creation stories of other cultures or multiple versions of one Native nation's creation story. They will begin to understand this idea and how this idea clouds understanding of Native cultures. Asking about one of something in relation to Native cultures cannot yield an appropriate or culturally accurate response.

Many indigenous cultures have a paired universe; life is understood to come in twos, not ones. There is a lengthy discussion of this on page 54 in *Land of the Three Miamis* by Mann, which is listed as a required text for use in the Native Women's Studies classroom. What ancient indigenous peoples from some nations saw in this world is that it is split in pairs and that this is the way our planet keeps herself in balance. For example, the ancients saw that this world is made of earth and sky, water and air, day and night, winter and summer, women and men, and elders and youths (*Native Americans, Archaeologists*...176). Because of their observations, their social and governing structures were created to reflect this balance. All manner of lawmaking, keeping time, keeping records, and life in general were centered around the notion of pairing. Anything that was a "one" was immediately suspect because it did not have its paired half to keep it in balance and therefore could potentially disrupt the community's balance (173). In the Eastern Woodlands, paired councils (one of only women and one of only men) governed their nations. Many traditional indigenous nations were structured by gender complementarity.

Sexual identification does not have bearing on the gendered halves practice of some Native nations. Students may inquire about where lesbians and gay men fit into the gendered halves social construction. Being gay, transgendered, or a hermaphrodite were not causes for social and religious persecution as they are in western culture, as all Native people were keenly aware of everyone belonging to the community despite clearly developing personal autonomy. More about sexualities is discussed in subsequent chapters.

Cultural Notions of Power

Power does not have a universal meaning, but it is based in cultural understanding. On the blackboard, overhead projector transparency, or the PowerPoint slide, the professor may write "Western Cultural Power," then ask the class the following question: "When someone in America has power, what do they have?" Some possible answers will be: lots of money, property/ land, influence laws, a good car, social status, special treatment by police, becoming a politician, and so on. Then ask students, "Who benefits from this person's power?" They will answer: the people they like, their kids, their wife (a telling response), a charity or college, and so on. What will be obvious in students' responses is the western cultural valuing of the self and that power is the accumulation of things for the self: all power is ultimately personal power.

Next, begin a discussion about Native power. From the previous lectures, students will already begin to differentiate between how indigenous people understand and express power and how westerners conceptualize and practice their understanding of it.

Ask the students, "In Native traditional cultures, who had power?" Most will say, "Everybody." Pressing them further, the professor may ask, "But what about leaders? We have not discussed governing structures in detail yet, but wouldn't the leaders have more power than the general population?" This line of questioning will make them thoughtful, and a few students may note that Native power is different from western power: Native "power" is really responsibility for looking after every one in the community; it is not about accumulation of things to promote the self. However, from course readings, students will find some instances of traditional Native nations where there was inequity of power.

In indigenous nations that had a gynocratic social system, power can best be translated to the notion of responsibility. Leaders were responsible for and to their nations: to ensure all citizens' basic needs were met and that they were protected under the law. Decisions made by governing bodies were for the perpetuation of the nation, not perpetuation of an individual's personal wealth or their friends' personal wealth. A position of leadership may have increased their social status to a position of honor, but this was not at the expense of other citizens. Nearly all Native nations held property, aside from one's personal possessions, in common. The earth was understood to be an entity with whom they were in relationship, and mindful use of her resources was indispensable, especially since misuse of her resources in the present generation might destroy future generations. Therefore, the accumulation of power via land ownership, personal wealth, and political gain generally did not exist for Native peoples in ways that they do for westerners. Capitalism based in land ownership was brought to the Americas by the settlers and did not exist here before the widespread practice of settler culture.

Course Texts

In choosing texts for the course the following guidelines should be kept in mind. First, texts written by Native American women are important to use. As you will soon come to understand, the cultural gap between Native and non-Native cultures is difficult to negotiate; hence, texts written by culturally identified Native American women, who have also gained traditional education (not merely western academic) from their Native community, will have a significant advantage over a text written by a non-Native academic. Cultural perspective is mandatory in the correct transmission of Native experience from instructor and texts to students.

One text for teaching a Native American Women's Studies class that should most certainly be on the course's required reading list is *The Sacred Hoop: Recovering the Feminine in American Indian Traditions* (1986) by Paula Gunn Allen. This book offers key theoretical and cultural perspectives on how Native women are understood within their culture, how that perspective has been changed via colonization, definitions, and practices of a gynocratic social system, and historic happenings affecting Native women's leadership today. Allen's landmark work will offer students a fundamental framework for understanding their subjects and for conducting appropriate research. *Grandmothers of the Light: A Medicine Woman's Sourcebook* (1991) is a work by Allen that expands on the theoretical work of *The Sacred Hoop* and is another possibility for inclusion in course readings.

Along with Allen's work, *Land of the Three Miamis* by Barbara Alice Mann, is a necessity in the Native Women's Studies classroom. The book offers in Native traditional narrative style a complete explanation of Eastern Woodlands culture, particularly outlining the work, duties, history, and cosmology of Native women. Mann engages a readily understandable manner of explaining complex cultural structures to the reader, and students appreciate the clear illustrations of a gendered society that can be hard to grasp for westerners to whom a paired universe is utterly foreign. The work is a slim volume best used at the beginning of the semester to introduce students to Eastern Native culture, a culture that has fundamental similarities to many indigenous nations in the Americas.

Required Texts

The Sacred Hoop: Recovering the Feminine in American Indian Traditions by Paula Gunn Allen. Boston: Beacon Press, 1986.

Land of the Three Miamis: A Traditional Narrative of the Iroquois by Barbara Alice Mann. Toledo, OH: University of Toledo Urban Affairs Center Press, 2006.

Along with these works outlining Native culture particularly relevant to Native women, an autobiographical work about a Native woman anchors and demonstrates cultural principles for students. An anthology of early and contemporary Native American women writers is also appropriate to include in the reading list, just as a biographical work about a Native woman can be informative and demonstrate contemporary cultural challenges of colonization of Native women. Some possibilities for additional required course reading may include the following books. This chronological list by publishing date is offered only as a guide not a prescription, though I have noted the books I strongly recommend; they are listed first.

Additional Required Reading Possibilities (Perhaps choose 3 from this list)

Spiderwoman's Granddaughters: Traditional Tales and Contemporary Writing by Native American Women by Paula Gunn Allen. Boston: Beacon Press, 1989. **Strongly recommended.

Tekonwatonti/Molly Brant/Poems of War by Maurice Kenny. Fredonia, NY: White Pine Press, 1992. **Strongly recommended.

Conquest: Sexual Violence and American Indian Genocide by Andrea Smith. Cambridge, MA: South End Press, 2005. **Strongly recommended.

American Indian Stories, Legends, and Other Stories by Zitkala-Sa, eds. Cathy N. Davidson and Ada Norris. New York: Penguin Books, 2003.

Pocahontas: Medicine Woman, Spy, Entrepreneur, Diplomat by Paula Gunn Allen. San Francisco: HarperSanFrancisco, 2003.

Medicine Trail: The Life and Lessons of Gladys Tantaquidgeon by Melissa Jayne Fawcett. Tucson: University of Arizona Press, 2000.

Woman of the Dawn by Bunny McBride. Lincoln: University of Nebraska Press, 1999.

Through the Eye of the Deer: An Anthology of Native American Women Writers, eds. Carolyn Dunn and Carol Comfort. San Francisco: Aunt Lute Books, 1999.

The Scalpel and the Silver Bear: The First Navajo Woman Surgeon Combines Western Medicine and Traditional Healing by Lori Arviso Alvord, M.D. and Elizabeth Cohen Van Pelt. New York: Bantam Books, 1999.

SELU: Seeking the Corn Mother's Wisdom by Marilou Awiakta. Golden, CO: Fulcrum Publishing, 1993.

Mankiller: A Chief and Her People—An Autobiography by the Principal Chief of the Cherokee Nation by Wilma Mankiller and Michael Wallis. New York: St. Martin's Press, 1993.

Grandmother's of the Light: A Medicine Woman's Sourcebook by Paula Gunn Allen. Boston: Beacon Press, 1991.

Lakota Woman by Mary Brave Bird (also authored under the name Mary Crow Dog) with Richard Erdoes. New York: HarperPerennial, 1991.

Halfbreed by Maria Campbell. Lincoln: University of Nebraska Press, 1982.

Recommended Supplemental and Research Works

I recommend selections from the following works for use as supplements to the course readings and as reference materials. Appropriate selections from them may be reproduced for the course with permission or held on reserve in your campus library for expansion on the topics concerning Native American women, historically and in contemporary times. Recommended works are listed below in chronological order, the most recent publication date listed first.

Sharing Our Stories of Survival: Native Women Surviving Violence, eds. Sarah Deer, et al. Lanham, MD: Altamira Press, 2008.

Indian Education in the American Colonies, 1607–1783 by Margaret Connell Szasz. Lincoln: University of Nebraska Press, 2007.

Native American Autobiography Redefined: A Handbook by Stephanie A. Sellers. New York: Peter Lang, 2007.

Grandmothers Counsel the World: Women Elders Offer Their Vision for Our Planet by Carol Schaefer, foreword by Winona LaDuke. Boston: Trumpeter, 2006.

Color of Violence: The Incite! Anthology by INCITE! Women of Color Against Violence. Cambridge, MA: South End Press, 2006.

Killing the Indian Maiden: Images of Native American Women in Film by M. Elise Marubbio. Lexington: University Press of Kentucky, 2006.

Daughters of Mother Earth, ed. Barbara Alice Mann. Westport, CT: Praeger, 2006.

Encyclopedia of Women and Religion in North America, eds. Rosemary Skinner Keller and Rosemary Radford Reuther, associate editor Marie Cantlon. Bloomington: Indiana University Press, 2006.

Cultural Representation In Native North America, ed. Andrew Jolivette. Lanham, MD: Altamira Press, 2006.

Reading Native American Women: Critical/Creative Representations, ed. Ines Hernandez-Avila. Lanham, MD: Altamira Press, 2005.

Recovering the Sacred: The Power of Naming and Claiming by Winona LaDuke. Cambridge, MA: South End Press, 2005.

Earth Democracy: Justice, Sustainability, and Peace by Vandana Shiva. Cambridge, MA: South End Press, 2005.

Undivided Rights: Women of Color Organize for Reproductive Justice, eds. Jael Silliman, et al. Cambridge, MA: South End Press, 2004.

Indigenous American Women: Decolonization, Activism, Empowerment by Devon Abbott Mihesuah. Lincoln: University of Nebraska Press, 2003.

Genocide of the Mind: New Native American Writing, ed. MariJo Moore. New York: Thunder's Mouth Press, 2003.

America's Second Tongue: American Indian Education and the Owner-ship of English, 1860–1900 by Ruth Spack. Lincoln: University of Nebraska Press, 2002.

Gay, Lesbian, Bisexual, and Transgender Myths from the Arapaho to the Zuni: An Anthology by Jim Elledge. New York: Peter Lang, 2002.

Sisters in Spirit: Haudenosaunee (Iroquois) Influence on Early American Feminists by Sally Roesch Wagner. Summertown, TN: Native Voices, 2001.

Learning to Be an Anthropologist and Remaining "Native": Selected Writings by Beatrice Medicine ed. with Sue-Ellen Jacobs. Urbana: University of Illinois Press, 2001

Native American Women: A Biographical Dictionary, 2nd edition, eds. Gretchen M. Bataille and Laurie Lisa. New York: Routledge, 2001.

Sifters: Native American Women Telling Their Lives, ed. Theda Per-due. Oxford: Oxford University Press, 2001.

Iroquoian Women: The Gantowisas by Barbara Alice Mann. Fore-word by Paula Gunn Allen. New York: Peter Lang, 2000.

Listening to Our Grandmother's Stories: The Bloomfield Academy for Chickasaw Females, 1852–1949 by Amanda J. Cobb. Lincoln: Uni-versity of Nebraska Press, 2000.

Women and Health in America: Historical Readings, ed. Judith Walzer Leavitt. Madison: University of Wisconsin Press, 1999.

All Our Relations, ed. Winona LaDuke. Cambridge, MA: South End Press, 1999.

Natives and Academics: Researching and Writing about American Indians, ed. Devon Mihesuah. Lincoln: University of Nebraska Press, 1998.

Men as Women, Women as Men: Changing Gender in Native American Cultures by Sabine Lang. Austin: University of Texas Press, 1998.

Two-Spirit People: Native American Gender Identity, Sexuality, and Spirituality, eds. Sue-Ellen Jacobs, et al. Urbana: University of Illinois Press, 1997.

Native American Women in Literature and Culture, eds. Susan Castillo and Victor M. P. DaRosa. Porto, Portugal: Fernando Pessoa University Press, 1997.

A Song to the Creator: Traditional Arts of Native American Women of the Plateau, ed. Lillian Ackerman. Norman: University of Oklahoma Press, 1996.

The Untold Story of the Iroquois Influence on Early Feminists by Sally Roesch Wagner. Aberdeen, UK: Sky Carrier Press, 1996.

Negotiators of Change: Historical Perspectives on Native American Women, ed. Nancy Shoemaker. New York: Routledge, 1995.

Women and Power in Native North America, eds. Laura F. Klein and Lillian Ackerman. Norman: University of Oklahoma Press, 1995. ** I recommend this work with caution as some selections take a biased, Eurocentric position.

Native Heritage: Personal Accounts by American Indians from 1790– present, ed. Arlene Hirschfelder. New York: Macmillan, 1995.

Women of the Native Struggle: Portraits and Testimony of Native American Women, ed. Ronnie Farley. New York: Orion Books, 1993.

Countering Colonization: Native American Women and Great Lakes Missions, 1630–1900 by Carol Devens. Berkeley: University of California Press, 1992.

American Indian Women: A Guide to Research, eds. Gretchen M. Bataille and Kathleen M. Sands. New York: Garland, 1991.

Mourning Dove: A Salishan Autobiography, ed. Jay Miller. Lincoln: University of Nebraska Press, 1990.

I Tell You Now: Autobiographical Essays by Native American Writers, eds. Arnold Krupat and Brian Swann. Lincoln: University of Nebraska Press, 1987.

That's What She Said: Contemporary Poetry and Fiction by Native American Women, ed. Rayna Greene. Bloomington: Indiana University Press, 1984.

Native American Women: A Contextual Bibliography by Rayna Green. Bloomington: Indiana University Press, 1983.

The Hidden Half: Studies of Plains Indian Women by Beatrice Medicine. Washington, D.C.: University Press of America, 1983.

These are just a few possibilities for supplemental course readings and research materials. There are many scholarly textbooks and anthologies of creative work written by or that discuss Native women's experiences with colonization and their identities within their nations. I have offered some choices on this subject to get teachers started, careful to select texts that clearly convey Native-centered points of view in order to prevent confusing students by texts that are misleading, Euro-centered scholarship.

In preparation for teaching the course, I strongly recommend that professors/workshop leaders read *Iroquoian Women: The Gantowisas* by Barbara Alice Mann. This is a dense, formidable text, definitive in its breadth of Eastern Woodlands epochal history and European colonization of northeastern North America and it places Native women in appropriate cultural context. The book is appropriate for upper-division undergraduate and graduate courses, and as a reference tool par excellence as it discusses non-Native primary sources over the past five hundred years relevant to understanding Native culture as well as strongly demonstrating Native cultural points of view. This book is not to be missed as it will lay the appropriate groundwork to successfully teach the class.

Relevant Journals for Use in Conducting Research and for Additional Course Readings

Affilia: Journal of Women & Social Work
Akwesasne Notes
American Anthropologist
American Historical Review
American Indian: Journal of the Smithsonian Museum of the American Indian
American Indian Culture & Research Journal
American Indian Literature and Critical Studies
American Indian Quarterly
American Institute of Indian Studies Quarterly Newsletter
Ethnohistory
Feminist Studies
Frontiers: A Journal of Women Studies
Indian Country Today (weekly newspaper)
Indian Life
Indigenous Nations Studies Journal
Indigenous Women's Magazine/Women of All Red Nations
Journal of Indian Family Research
Journal of Indigenous Studies
Journal of Women's History
Legacy: A Journal of American Women Writers
National Women's Studies Association Journal
North Dakota Quarterly
Signs: Journal of Women in Culture & Society

Social Science Journal
Studies in American Indian Literatures
Wicazo Sa Review
Women and Music: A Journal of Gender and Culture

The Research Project

A research paper is a requirement of my class as it teaches about the subject matter as well as gives students experience developing research skills.

Students are expected to narrow their research to a manageable focus, write a paper discussing the research and critically analyze it, include a correctly formatted works cited page, and present their research to the class. I allow up to two students to choose each topic. They cannot work together, but may present their research to the class together. Video excerpts from documentaries, films, or interviews are sometimes included in the presentations and should be encouraged. The presentations begin about a month into the semester and continue to the end of the term thus serving as important supplemental information to the course. Here are some suggestions for the research project about "Native American women":

- Forced sterilization of Native American women
- Political activists (sovereignty, repatriation, land rights, and so on)
- Patriarchal origins theories compared to a Native nation's gendered practices
- Issues around use of the term "squaw"
- Environmental activists
- Traditional artists/weavers/potters

- Pow-wow dancing and beading
- Critical review: Issues and strategies of cultural survivance
- Contemporary artists/weavers/potters challenging traditional forms
- Changing leadership roles in nations (precolonial models to contemporary times)
- Violence against Native women
- Settler primary sources: earliest writings about Native women
- Menarche/first moontime rituals
- Native women at the Smithsonian National Museum of the American Indian
- Warriors, generals, and soldiers during colonization
- American Indian Movement
- First Movers/Creators and their cosmologies
- Pregnancy and birth rituals
- Lesbianism in Native cultures
- Roles in the American suffragist movement
- Missionary school experiences
- Cherokee Female Seminary School
- Bloomfield Academy for Chickasaw females
- Experiences with colonial adoption practices of Native children
- Writers publishing before 1900
- Writers publishing after 1900
- Presented in film
- Gynocracy and ecofeminism movement
- In the academy (faculty, students, and pertinent issues)

Biographical Project and Presentation

Early in the semester I require students to conduct research and present it to the class in groups about one Native American woman. The presentations are given serially (about two per class) and completed within a two week period. The objective of this project is to introduce students to Native culture and offer them an in-depth opportunity to read about the historic role, activism, literary work, or art of a Native woman and then offer a teaching to the class. This project often opens the eyes of students about the important roles Native women have held/still hold in American society and moves them from margin to center in the students' eyes. Most students have never heard of any of the Native women on the biography list, except for Pocahontas and Sacajawea, and what they know about them is limited.

In groups of three, I allow students to choose from a list of Native women stated on the syllabus by due date and present their research to the class via use of technology (PowerPoint presentation). Samples of artwork can be shown on the slide show, music can be played, and samples of literature and teachings can be read aloud to the class. Expecting the student audience to sing along, dance, or enact an historic scene often happens and is welcome! Many times a rereading of the speech given by Zitakala-Ša at the infamous state oratory contest has been interrupted by a (secretly selected) student audience member holding up the racist sign Zitkala-Ša had to face—to the shock of the class. Students sometimes dress the part and take on the persona of a Native woman and present a dramatic, biographical work in character. Artistic works are not uncommon as: short stories written in the voice of the Native woman being researched and even a contemporary rap song noting the life of the Native woman have been presented to delighted students (and me) in past classes. What is learned from this project is not soon forgotten by students. Encourage students to be creative!

Some Native women I have asked student groups to research include the three women just mentioned, Pretty-Shield, Bunny McBride, Mourning Dove, Sarah Winnemucca, Mabel McKay, E. Pauline Johnson, Grace Thorpe, Mary TallMountain, Winona La-Duke, Wilma Mankiller, Buffy St. Marie, Joanne Shenandoah, Elizabeth Cook-Lynn, and Mary Brave Bird. Of course, there are many others to choose from. The presentation should include:

- Biographical information including information about her nation
- Role the individual played(s) in her nation
- Role the individual played(s) in American history
- A representative sample of the woman's words or music or artwork
- Photographs or drawings of the woman from books or an electronic source
- Video or film clip about or of her

Students enjoy this project immensely and the overall class benefits significantly from the presentations.

Conclusion

These beginning lectures initiate students to the rudimentary beliefs and practices of some Native cultures that will be expanded upon in course readings and student research. At the onset, some students may have a conflict of allegiance with western culture, their upbringing, and their religious beliefs, which professors might address by noting that the course does not seek right/wrong, either/or thinking. Doing so is not scholarly. Indeed, multiple, cultural perspectives is the premise of the course. Internal conflict can be addressed through the "checking-in" practice held at the beginning of class perhaps once a week. In this exercise, students have the opportunity to talk about feelings the course materials are invoking in them and can then process any conflict there may be. While sitting in a circle, the professor/leader may begin the class discussion by asking about how students are reacting to what they are learning in the course: how they feel, what they may have shared with their friends and family and how those individuals are responding, and so on. At the beginning of the course, there will be plenty of feedback!

Sample Proposal Form for Teaching This Course
at a College

1. Course Description

Native American Women. Interdisciplinary exploration on how indigenous women, primarily from gynocratic nations, were conceptualized and functioned within their nations from pre-colonization to contemporary times. Cultural notions of power and gender discussed and how they shape indigenous social and governing structures. Traditional customs concerning sexuality, marriage, and reproduction are contrasted with western cultural prescriptions for women. Ways in which indigenous women and men balance the responsibilities of their nation are a key topic.

2. Course Overview

Native American Women will introduce students to the ancient
indigenous sociopolitical practice that makes women's leadership in the Eastern Woodlands and other gynocratic nations central in Native American national decision making. The power of
self-determination for women within the bounds of communal
ethics is a key theme of the course, and the rituals and cosmology that govern that right are discussed. How indigenous
women negotiate identity, maintain the spiritual health and survival of their nations, and keep their traditional practices alive
today are also topics. The impact of colonization on Native
women is a key theme as well.

A possible reading list would likely include:

*The Sacred Hoop: Recovering the Feminine in American Indian
Traditions* by Paula Gunn Allen.
This text offers Native North American historical background in
relation to women's ritual and offers definitive and theoretical
discussions about gynocratic sociopolitical structures (a woman-
centered governing body). The Eastern Woodlands people are
one of many Native nations who were/are gynocratic.

Tekonwatonti/Molly Brant/Poems of War by Maurice Kenny.
An award-winning poetry collection in the voices of Mohawk
clan mother (1736-1796) and her community. An indigenous
historic perspective.

Land of the Three Miamis by Barbara Alice Mann.

Epochal history of the Iroquois presented in a traditional narrative style. Explanation of gendered halves principles of culture.

Spiderwoman's Granddaughters by Paula Gunn Allen.
An anthology of ancient, traditional, and contemporary stories by Native American women. Creation stories and issues of colonization discussed.

Prerequisites: None

Contact Hours: 3

Course Requirements for Students and Criteria for Evaluation (Including Final Examination or Its Equivalent):

Course Requirements:
1. Group biographical project presented to class using technology;
2. Two academic papers based in part on research and on learning from course texts;
3. One personal reflective paper about the student's cultural experience as a woman (or about a woman relative if the student is male);
4. Meaningful class participation that demonstrates close interaction with course texts and themes of course.
5. One mid-term.
6. One research paper and presentation.

Criteria for Evaluation:

1. 40% of the grade is based on paper writing;
2. 10% on the group biographical project;
3. 20% on the midterm;
4. 10% on class participation;
5. 20% on the research paper.

Limits on Student Enrollment: 30

3. Goals and Competencies

Summarize your goals for students and the competencies the course is designed to help them develop:

Goals

To expose students to the gynocentric sociopolitical structures of Native North Americans, particularly the Eastern Woodlands peoples.

To make students aware of gender-specific modes of thinking and ways of being, and how indigenous ways are radically different from western cultural ways.

To challenge students' understanding of the notions of gender and power, and how these notions are shaped by a nation's cosmology.

To personally empower women students with the knowledge that many of the original inhabitants of what is now called America were woman-centered, woman-governed peoples, devoid of oppression and violence against women, and that all American women can reap the wisdom of that legacy.

Competencies

By the end of the course, students will have learned to:

- Recognize complex cultural and philosophical differences between Indigenous ways of knowing and western cultural ones in relation to perceptions of women.
- Feel confident about their level of knowledge concerning the sociopolitical structure of some gynocentric indigenous nations.
- Understand the concept that cosmology plays a role in shaping human beliefs about gender and power, and their relationship to each other.
- Understand the Native-defined relationship between women and the earth, and how being female offers a position of power and, therefore, duty to one's entire community.
- Challenge their own culturally defined identity as women (or their perceptions of women) and, perhaps, think of themselves in a changed, more positive, and empowered, way.

4. Curricular Issues

a. *Will this course meet any requirements for the department or program major and/or minor? Please explain:*

Yes. This course will meet the Diversity requirement (both nonwestern and Domestic/Conceptual) of the new curriculum. Ways in which the course will meet these requirements are:

- the course will expose students to the history and culture of non-western cultural peoples living within the geographical boundaries of the United States;
- it will offer a non-Eurocentric point of view of the colonization of the United States;
- it will offer description of how Native women negotiate identity, maintain their traditions, and live within the broader cultural context called "America" since colonization.

b. *Does this course fit into a sequence?*

No.

c. *Why is the course assigned to this level?*

The 200 level is assigned because course requirements and reading expectations are beyond the introductory level.

d. *How does this course connect to other parts of the curriculum? Are there other courses that it complements?*

This course may encourage students to seek a major or minor in women's studies, interdisciplinary studies, or history.

CHAPTER III

Women's Studies Terminology and Concepts from a Native Perspective

This chapter will address the challenges of teaching, thinking, and speaking about Native American women in the Women's Studies classroom. We academics tend to believe that the theories, terms, and concepts we have invented in our various disciplines are universal and entirely definitive. Perhaps they can be generally and appropriately applied in most experiments, criticism, and research in the academy in relation to matters of western culture. However, as a general rule, they cannot be applied when discussing, evaluating, and interrogating any indigenous culture. The rules change altogether when we move from one culture to another. Biologically there is much sameness among human races and ethnic groups, but that is where the sameness ends. There is no universal application across the myriad human cultures of the theories and terminology created in western culture from the social sciences and humanities disciplines. Feminist scholars readily acknowledge the multiplicity of perspectives and epistemologies apparent in various cultures and feminisms; however, this approach often fails within other disciplines. Therefore, the pages that follow will offer guidelines in moving from a western theoretical and terminological approach and practices in Women's Studies to a Native one. Doing so successfully in the college classroom, or with professionals who have an academic background in a women's advocacy group, poses significant challenges. Students will wish to return to labeling Native social structures, spiritual practices, and understanding gender with western, academic terms and perceptions. It is the job of the teacher to guide them away from doing so.

Though Native American scholars write and speak extensively to inform and request that non-Native academics cease using western cultural ideologies, terms, and metaphors to describe Native cultures, western academics often still continue to do so. This is called ethnocentrism, a culturally delegitimizing practice that is unethical. For example, Native scholars note that the structures of indigenous gendering are deliberate replications of the cosmos, but non-Native academics routinely call them "divisions of labor" or "gender roles" and insist that they are the result of events for which anthropologists and feminists have invented categories and terminology. Please avoid this practice in your classroom. The practice is a clear statement that the academics "really know" what the Natives were/are doing and that they, the Natives themselves, simply cannot recognize it or properly name it—or worse, Natives are simply mistaken about their own history and culture and Native academics are misguided and biased reporters. This, by the way, is called racism, though it seems all too often "only natural" to some academics to make such claims.

We would never say that journalists living in New York City are not qualified to report on national events or New York life because they are New Yorkers or Americans. Additionally, academics would never claim that Anglo-American male professors are not qualified to teach and write about Shakespeare because they would be biased or unprofessional since they are the same gender and race. Academics understand that true professionals have high ethical standards. This expectation holds true for all human races and ethnicities in and out of academia. Therefore, Native academics are just as qualified to study their own or other Native cultures just as any American academic can be qualified to study American culture. This may seem like an obvious observation, but unfortunately Native academics often still experience significant criticism from non-Native colleagues when they write and teach about their own culture.

The Creation Story Sets the Gendering Stage

One of the first reading assignments on my syllabus includes the creation story of the Eastern Woodlands people. This is the story of Sky Woman, the Lynx, the Twins, and the animals who created Turtle Island: the First Family. The story sets the cultural philosophy foundation of the course, and I refer to it throughout the semester. Since it is a story, students can remember its concepts well; this is one reason why the Native ancestors created and ritually repeat it. It is a micro-representation of the entire Eastern Woodlands cultural philosophy. Cosmological stories demonstrate foundational beliefs of a people and can be used to direct students to understanding complex cultural concepts.

Through the creation story students are introduced to a few new concepts: a woman creator is centralized, all the participants in the story are cooperative creators (even the animals), and gender pairing and complementarity are demonstrated. Both Mann's and Allen's texts (*Land of the Three Miamis* and *The Sacred Hoop*, respectively) discuss the story and its cultural meaning. Mann's is highly detailed, and I assign her version during the second class of the semester. First, what is primary for the instructor of the course to emphasize is that the Twins, sons of the Lynx, are NOT metaphors of good and evil. The notions of "good and evil" are inventions of western culture and have no application to most indigenous cultures and their cosmologies. It is important for the instructor to steer students firmly away from this dichotomization of the Twins, as it is entirely Eurocentric. The notions that one "good" spirit (the monotheistic God) is fighting with one "bad" spirit (the devil) and influencing human behavior and thinking is an invention of western culture and has no correlation in many traditional indigenous cultures. Claiming that the good/evil notions are universal to humanity is ethnocentrism. See page 71 of Mann's *Iroquoian Women: The Gantowisas* for a full discussion of this topic.

Second, just as Sky Woman and the Lynx are centralized in the story, so are women in general in Eastern Woodlands culture as is true for gynocratic indigenous cultures. Indeed, as Mann notes, this is the very principle that created women's sole right to the distribution of the bounty of Mother Earth, to naming, and to maintaining the chief lineage rights. The introduction of Sky

Woman can be a powerful experience for some students, though the notion of a single male god will most likely be deeply ingrained in them. Some may feel empowered, while others may feel threatened by this knowledge and seek to either discount it as an untrue "primitive invention" or myth, or they may focus on the male Twins as the primary creators. Allowing for open discussion about their experiences with the creation story helps to alleviate their resistance and give an opportunity for expressing their mind-opening excitement or conflict (sometimes created by discussion with their parents).

Third, communal ethics are introduced in the creation story, just as the equitable inclusion of the actions of the animals is also included. Again, this will be a new concept: working together without competition. Remind them about the Hierarchy of Existence model previously discussed, noting that the animals are equal members of the community; humans are not "above" them in importance.

I have offered analysis of the Iroquoian creation story that demonstrates a gender complementary system, but there are many other creation stories professors may wish to choose. Be advised though that versions of the stories should come from reputable sources as there are many Euroformed versions available that either focus entirely on a singular male creator, are Christianized versions of traditional stories, or they have written out women creators altogether. If any of these elements are present in the story, find a more culturally accurate model for the class to read.

Feminism

Feminism is a term invented by the academy and is a practice that supports the social and economic empowerment of women. It is often based in conflict between women and men. Feminism has little application in traditional Native cultures and this is why: Native women do not fight ending oppression for themselves, but for their people. They do not see themselves as entities separate from their men, their nation, the earth, or their children. They do not fight for women's rights, but for communal rights, and community means Mother Earth and all her creatures. Indigenous nations were primarily based in gender complementarity or gender balance. There is no framework in western culture for this notion. Gender conflict is embedded in western culture and perpetuated by its religions and social structures. This is why feminism as a notion and a practice was created and enacted in western culture; women had to find a way out of their paralyzing cultural predicament.

Second, feminism was initially a result of the conflict between women and men because women in western culture have been horribly disenfranchised: murdered by the scores during the European witch hunts, oppressed in their monotheistic religions, and barred from educational, economic, political, and social opportunity—even unto today. Unfortunately, most of the earliest written texts that shaped western culture espoused degradation of women and supported a social structure that continues to keep them oppressed. This is not the history of indigenous women of the Eastern Woodlands and most other indigenous nations of the Americas. Only after colonization began did the sexism of western culture start to permeate the cultures of Natives and contaminate the equitable systems that had been in place for thousands of years.

Now in contemporary times Native women are often horribly oppressed within their nations and are particularly targets for sexual violence by both Native and non-Native men. The brand of suffering that only women from western culture had to bear for millennia has now come to Turtle Island with the settlers: rape, violence in the home, and political disenfranchisement have found the former national leaders of the gynocratic indigenous nations. Nevertheless, when Native women step forward to disband these atrocities, they are not feminists: they are Native women merely doing what their ancestors would expect. Their job is to protect the current and rising generations of their people, protect their culture, and protect the entire biosphere.

Note that feminism is about women getting ahead of or catching up to men or stepping out from the confines of restriction set on women of western culture. However, *indigenous women seek to restore gender balance to their nations to reconnect with their traditions, which is the cultural strength of their people.* Herein is the significant difference between feminism and the actions of empowerment of Native women: one centralizes the self or only other women and the other is communal and based on ancient tradition.

Ecofeminism

This term was coined during the early days of feminism and is linked with the environmental protection movement. Ecofeminism addresses the relationship between social domination, particularly oppression of women, and the abuse of nature. Ecofeminists discuss the connection between the antienvironment bases of western culture: patriarchy, Christianity, and capitalism. Abuse of the earth is another misogynist practice of western culture: acts of hatred and exploitation of the environment are linked with acts of hatred and exploitation of women. Ecofeminists argue that the earth and women are both perceived as merely objects to use by the institutions of western culture and our current state of environmental crisis (particularly its impact on women's health with the record high incidence of breast, cervical, and ovarian cancers) demonstrates this connection. Further, supporters of this movement add that the cruel ways in which animals are treated in commercial slaughter houses reflect the western cultural disconnection from the plight of the living. The nationally recognized scholar and feminist, Mary Daly, notes in her book *Gyn/Ecology* that western culture is a culture that values and perpetuates death.

Ecofeminism is one term and concept of western culture that does have an appropriate application in Native culture because Native nations were, in some ways, the original ecofeminists. Of course, the principles of ecofeminism are built directly into the ethics, creation stories, traditions, and communal practices of many Native nations since the beginning of time. Honoring the earth and women were centralized concepts and practices of many Native nations; the evidence of this is demonstrated in the volumes of indigenous creation stories and in their national practices.

Prohibition of harm to women, children, the earth, and her animals is clearly demonstrated in many Native creation stories. For example, in the ancient Eastern Woodlands story of the Sacred Twins, Flint played a trick on his brother Sapling by trapping all the forest animals. When Sapling discovered this, he freed the animals (*Land of the Three*...30). This story cautions against fencing in animals, a practice seldom done by Native nations before colonization. Indeed, when the peoples of the east discovered that the European settlers fenced in their animals and so cruelly treated them (branding them, beating them, forcing them to stand in their own feces, then butchering them without ceremony or prayer), they were horrified at this cruelty.

To both ecofeminists and Native American nations, the acts of barbarism against women, children, and the earth are certainly connected. All of such actions demonstrate a principle of violence and an utter disregard for the next generations, a principle that is abhorrent and astounding to indigenous nations without exception.

Archetypes

The well-known scholar of modern psychology, Carl Jung, wrote extensively about archetypes connecting them with human personality, mental disorders, and behaviors. His predecessor, Sigmund Freud, had a similar approach in his works. These archetypes were based on western cultural family models, Greek mythology, and perceptions about gender. From beginning to end, Jung's work is entirely embedded in the belief systems and worldview of western culture; therefore, as you can well imagine by now, they have no appropriate application to indigenous cultures. Archetype theory cannot be universally applied. Unfortunately, Jung himself, as well as most contemporary sociologists, anthropologists, and psychologists, assert that his archetypes are universal; that all human beings can fit into certain categories or roles and will respond to certain situations, stimuli, and relationships in similar ways. Barbara Mann offers a Native critique of "archetalk" in her *Iroquoian Women: The Gantowisas* (62, 326).

I will elaborate here on only one example that will demonstrate the enormous disparity between Native and western culture when applying Jungian archetype theory. One of Jung's archetypes include the Mother archetype, but this is the Mother under the western cultural model, not the indigenous one. Mother is understood in terms of how westerners understand women, the identity of a woman who has birthed a child, the relationship of that woman to the child, and the relationship of the woman to the man with whom she has created the child. The Mother archetype to westerners is woman as either the benign Nurturer or the malevolent Destroyer (primarily of sons). There is antagonism toward the self and toward all men built into this archetype. The Mother has no political, economic, or social status; she is merely a reproducer who then interacts with the human she has reproduced. The western definition of the Mother archetype stops there.

To indigenous peoples the Mother archetype does not by any means exist in the manner Jung has shaped it. To Eastern Woodlands peoples, mother means the person who holds a position of psychospiritual, economic, social, and political power—not a woman who has merely biologically reproduced! Indeed, even a man, albeit with a lot of work, could be referred to by the honorific Mother. *Mother* is a term connoting communal responsibility for the perpetuation of the nation and all its sustenance—spiritual, physical, emotional, and psychological. Mother, via the clan mothers' council, is also the person who has the first and the final word on all matters brought before lawmaking bodies: local and federal. Further, Mother is a general term of respect that is independent of biological reproduction and can be used to address any woman who has begun her menstrual cycle in order to be respectful toward her. Grandmother is an even higher term of respect.

The archetypes of western culture do not apply to indigenous cultures and should not be used as a framework to understand Native women, or Native men for that matter. The epistemologies of western culture are appropriate and useful for the things of that culture, but they have no value whatsoever in any discussion about Native culture and should not be used other than to draw broad cultural distinctions between the two cultural worldviews. How *Mother* is defined in traditional indigenous cultures varies from nation to nation, and the term has been drastically changed by settler beliefs that were promulgated via religious texts and social practices over the past five hundred years.

Menstruation

Menarche, or the first menstrual cycle of a woman, is a sacred time in the life of a Native girl. With this physical experience comes a time of deep spiritual searching and a heightened sense of duty to one's community. This is a time when the girl moves into not only womanhood but motherhood. However, this perception is not based on biological reproduction, but on her future roles in her nation as political, spiritual, and economic leader.

Women's monthly bleeding is called her "moontime" in some Native nations. As Barbara Mann notes, this is women's connection with Our Grandmother the Moon (Sky Woman) and the moon's own monthly cycles. Just as the moon fills with light every month, women too fill with blood, then move into a period of darkness or emptiness. There are various ceremonies and sacred traditions around the bleeding and nonbleeding times of women across the Native nations and throughout the world's traditional cultures. Students will read about some of these traditions in Allen's *The Sacred Hoop*.

In many Native nations, at the first moontime there will be particular rituals and ceremonies held for the girl and these vary widely from nation to nation, though there is most often singing and feasting by her clan members (female and male), and a period of solitude and prayer for the girl. At this time, she is encouraged to discover the purposes of her life and to then seek ways to fulfill those purposes. She may receive a new name or a spiritual name (kept secret) then as well. During subsequent bleeding until she becomes a grandmother (goes through menopause), she will spend her monthly menses alone, nourishing herself and refraining from her daily duties at a special location. The menstrual cycle of a woman is understood by Natives to be a time of exceptional power and this is why Native women secluded themselves—so they did not counteract another's work with her heightened power brought on via her menstrual cycle.

When one looks at the absence of rituals and the deeply shaming beliefs in western culture relating to women's menstrual blood, it is easy to recognize how women are perceived because of their gender. Even the cycles of women's bodies are not respected in contemporary western culture. From secrecy to fear of blood stains on clothing, women of western culture are taught to hide and be ashamed of their menstrual blood and to never discuss it openly, particularly in front of men. It is called "the curse" or said that a woman is "on the rag" when she is bleeding. There are bumper stickers for automobiles that read "I don't trust anything that can bleed for three days and not die." Overall, the menstrual cycle in western culture is something that is feared and used against women to make them feel unbalanced and incompetent, especially during the cycle itself. The cycle is often perceived as an interruption of a woman's daily life, and medical treatments have been invented to suppress or even end monthly bleeding. Contemporary Native elders have noted that the suffering of premenstrual syndrome is a result of modern women not being allowed to care for themselves during their cycles.

Female Stages of Life

In the Eastern Woodlands and in many other Native cultures, a female human's identity is based on her bodily functions, and these functions have connections to her political roles. A female Native person is a girl until she begins her moon cycle. After that, she is considered a Woman who is moving toward becoming a Mother. As I have already discussed, Mother means a person who cares politically, economically, spiritually, and physically for her nation; it does not solely mean she has reproduced. Paula Gunn Allen's book *Grandmothers of the Light* (noted in the bibliography in chapter two) notes many more stages, like Healer and Cultivator. A female stays in the Woman/Mother stage of her life until she becomes a Grandmother; this means her moon cycles have stopped. The Grandmother stage is a time of particular power, especially political and spiritual power in many nations.

Note the following from these stages: they are not based in sexuality or in any relationship to men. Native women's stages of life and the subsequent social opportunities attributed to those stages are based and contained solely in their bodies' cycles. These functions are also not merely biological, but they are considered to be deeply spiritual and connected to the larger cosmos. They are indeed reflections of the cosmos.

Sexual expression occurs at the time and frequency deemed appropriate for the young woman by the young woman herself. She is encouraged to know her body and to grow in maturity as she moves through adulthood. In the Eastern Woodlands and many other Native nations, multiple partners were expected before marriage. Same-sex partnering was not condemned.

In the western cultural model, the stages of women's lives are embedded in heterosexual relationships with men. Young females are indeed also referred to as girls, just as in the Native model, but they are also called virgins and maidens (asexual relationship to men). If there are so-called "inappropriate" or "excessive" sexual relationships to men, young women of western culture are called demeaning names like sluts and whores. Young women engaging in same-sex relationships are called demeaning names such as dyke or man-hater, among others. Certain types of sexual expression may bar women from future opportunities of heterosexual marriage and create social ostracism.

In western culture, only women who have biologically reproduced are called mothers. A woman can only be a grandmother if her offspring has also reproduced. Being a mother and a grandmother does not afford women any special political, social, or economic power; indeed, an aging woman in western culture is most often discriminated against in those very categories because youth and youthful appearance are rewarded in women. A physical appearance of inexperience is deemed attractive in women of western culture.

Gender Roles

The phrase *gender roles* is an academic term of western culture created by feminists and social scientists. It is based on the observation that women's and men's biological make-up determines what duties they will perform in the home and which responsibilities they will hold in the larger social structure. For example, in western culture women have historically been unpaid homemakers and men have worked for pay outside the home in careers. Another example would be that women cook the dinner and do the dishes, and men take out the trash. Of course, these roles can vary widely from home to home and have changed somewhat over the decades from the pre-World War II model. Nevertheless, culturally these roles are embedded into the social structure of western culture. For further amplification: As a very telling reversal of gender roles, the front page artwork of the 2005 Thanksgiving issue of *The New Yorker* showed women and girls sitting around the television in a living room rooting for a football team, while men and boys wore aprons and filled the kitchen working on the Thanksgiving dinner.

Gender roles have deep psychological meaning and values attached to them. Women's work in the home is understood to be less important than men's work outside the home. Women are not paid money for their work, and they are seldom recognized for it as professionals outside the home are given promotions, raises, and awards. Also, by being kept working in the home, women have been barred from playing leadership roles in the governing and economic rules of their culture. This structure further disenfranchises them because they are then told they are not capable of being leaders and policy makers.

In indigenous nations, there are no gender roles. The complementary gendering of the Eastern Woodlands, and many other Native nations, is based on the deliberate re-creation of the cosmos—it is spiritual, cosmological, and reflects the balance of the biosphere. Native people noted how this world keeps herself in balance and deliberately created a system that would reflect that balance in order to ensure their human structure would be viable and healthy. Native women had/have their responsibilities to the nation just as the men did/do. In the East, women were Keepers of the Earth and men were Keepers of the Forest. Barbara Mann discusses this complex Native concept and the correlating practices in her *Iroquoian Women: The Gantowisas*, chapter "The Direction of the Sky: Gendered for Balance," beginning page 58. I recommend a close study of this entire chapter.

The important point to note is that Eastern Woodlands' Native women's work in the home is understood to be local politics, though their power in federal matters was unquestionable, not housecleaning and dishes! Further, how the interior work of women balanced the exterior work of men varied with each indigenous nation and was not always equitable. In the Eastern Woodlands, working in the "home" did not bar women from having their own councils and holding all male chief lineages or any other duties deemed "outside the home sphere" or "male" in western culture. In other words, women's work in Native nations was often on par with men's work; indeed, to hold one above the other would mean upsetting the careful balance they maintained to keep their nation and the biosphere healthy.

Though women in many precolonial Native societies had their duties and men had theirs, in some of those nations people could also aspire to serve in their opposite gender capacities if so inclined. The gender complementary responsibilities in Native cultures were often not unalterable prescriptions, but were geared to maintain balance, not to oppress one gender over the other.

Essentialism

Another academic term that we use in the Women's Studies discipline is essentialism. Essentialism is the notion that a woman (or man) is not defined merely by their biological composition. It is based less on biology than on perceptions that certain characteristics of women and men adhere to certain gender groups naturally. For example, essentialism is a belief that women are by nature more caretaking and men are by nature more aggressive. These beliefs are then applied to social constructions that claim women are naturally or organically better at raising children and working in the home and men are naturally better at being political leaders and heads of commerce.

In the Native model, biology does play a role in defining gender, but gender is understood to be far more complex. "Woman" is seen as *one of* the balancing principles of the cosmos and *one way* that this principle is expressed is through human biology. See Mann's *Iroquoian Women: The Gantowisas*, beginning page 97, for a detailed discussion. However, there are also many other ways "woman" is expressed in the biosphere and within a woman's, or man's, life. For example, the woman principle of this biosphere is also expressed in earth and water, in winter and in turtle, in the Pleiades and in the plants. These are not mere metaphors, but literal expressions of the paired/twinned principles of this world as Eastern Woodlanders see it; each Native nation has their own expressions for this concept. Men can become women politically and act within the capacity of women, as judges and lawmakers. Therefore, the labels of "woman" and "man" could be transcended through political and social promotion because the labels themselves are only partly based in biology.

Further, both women and men in gynocratic nations were understood to be nurturers of children and also to be leaders among a myriad of other duties to the nation. Achieving the highest *human* principles was a goal expected of all people; human ideals were not applied by gender, though they were often expressed via practices based in gender. This is only one of the staggering differences between understanding women and men in gynocratic nations versus the nations of western culture.

Homosexuality

As any casual observer of western culture, particularly contemporary culture, can discern, humans who have same-sex orientation for sexual or long-term relationships are generally mistreated, sometimes violently so. Gay people are denied equal citizenship in our society in a variety of ways and must often hide their identity in fear of ostracism. Religious groups in western culture often publicly condemn gay people and bar them from participation in religious worship and leadership roles. In western contemporary culture, being a lesbian woman or a gay man carries with it a variety of difficult challenges that create significant suffering for them from childhood to adulthood.

In many traditional Native societies, being homosexual was not an issue. Homosexual deities and archetypes (Native ones) are featured in creation and other traditional stories. See the Recommended Reading list for a text on these stories. Condemning people for their personal preferences was typically not a practice of indigenous peoples because setting prescriptions for life was considered wrong: every person was expected to find his or her own personal purpose in life and seek to fulfill that purpose. As long as the purpose supported communal ethics (responsibility to the nation), the purpose was not anyone else's business.

Conclusion

Teaching a course in Native American Women's Studies requires redefining the terms we use in the Women's Studies discipline and shaping them to expand, not obscure, cultural meaning. Some terms must be abandoned altogether as they simply have no application outside western culture.

CHAPTER IV

Native American Terminology for the Women's Studies Classroom

Teaching across cultures requires not only reexamination of the terminology and theories professors already use in Women's Studies or their chosen field, but it also necessitates learning entirely new terms and ways of understanding human social structures. This chapter prepares instructors for understanding and explaining to students key concepts and terms that will be discussed throughout the Native American Women's Studies course. Most of these concepts and terms are expounded upon in the required texts I have already noted. Some, on the other hand, are not directly discussed, or direct linkages and comparisons to western cultural structures and history are not elaborated upon as much as might be helpful to the instructor venturing into this field for the first time. Therefore, this chapter should serve as a navigational tool and a quick reference guide to fundamental concepts and histories relevant in the Native Women's Studies classroom.

Gynocracy

This term is introduced in Allen's text *The Sacred Hoop* where she discusses histories and characteristics of Native gynocracies. A gynocracy is a woman-centered governing system: gyno (meaning woman) and cracy (meaning government or type of government rule). Though woman-centered, it does not disenfranchise men, the earth's resources, or any group's autonomy. Indeed, as Allen explains in the book's Introduction, a primary goal of a gynocracy is to create mutuality, live without punitiveness, demonstrate communal ethics, and live in balance (2-3). Balance means living with mindfulness to the earth so that the future of the people is not left in peril. It means consensus decision making that can be at times fraught with conflict, though conflict is expressed and understood in a manner wholly different from western culture. To some matrilineal peoples, conflict is utterly abhorrent and is avoided at all costs: Decisions are made without expressing conflict even if opinions vary widely.

Gender Complementary Structures

The Eastern Woodlands peoples, the Iroquois or Haudenosaunee, are a gynocratic nation. What is primary in their governing system is that the balance between clan mothers and male sachems, between women's and men's councils, was set by the re-creation of the cosmos by the originators of this structure (the ancestors). They understand the world to be twinned or paired, as discussed earlier, and therefore their government reflects this worldview. Though women have the first and last word on governing and decision making, the men also have a say. The men are not silenced or oppressed. Their role is to balance the decisions of the women by providing in-put in the decision making process, carrying out those decisions (by going to war, for example), and representing their nation in federal matters through acts of diplomacy and negotiation. Balance is maintained, for that is how the nation continues.

One gender group having primary power in a social structure that is used to erase, silence, or control the other gender group is not present in a gynocratic social structure. The reason oppression of one gender is not present is because gynocratic structures, though woman-based and woman-centered, are *based on balance of genders, not supremacy of women*. This is a pivotal point to emphasize to students. Women are centralized in most indigenous cultures because they are central in their nation's creation stories, and because women are central in the perpetuation of the nation via biological, spiritual, and psychological sustenance for the people. Observing women's obvious centrality, indigenous nations arranged their governments and social structures to reflect this reality for the perpetuation of their descendants. Even so, in some gender complementary indigenous systems, women did not enjoy the same freedoms that men did.

The patriarchal or male-lineage model that western culture functions under does indeed oppress the other gender, women, as this model is based not on gender complementarity but on a hierarchical structure. This patriarchal structure supports social, economic, and political power in the hands of a few people (primarily light-skinned males) and the majority of the people (especially women, people of color, nonheterosexuals) are in a disenfranchised position that often transcends race, gender, and ethnicity.

In other words, even if a Native American woman becomes a professional and makes an upper-middle-class salary, she will still be discriminated against in her daily life because of her gender, skin color, and ethnicity. The patriarchal structure does not support what Natives would consider an appropriate relationship with the earth, so that relationship too is out of balance. The patriarchal model is a "top down" social structure based in the supremacy of light-skinned males, and the gynocratic social structure is a "half & half" social structure based in gender complementarity.

Matrilineal Descent

Matrilineal descent is a feature of a gynocracy; this means that a child's clan and physical home is determined by the mother's clan lineage and home. Within a matrilineal structure, when a couple marries, the man comes to live with his wife's clan, and if there is a divorce, the man returns to his mother's home. Children are never taken away from their mother via male custody due to a divorce. Children are understood to belong to their mother, though the father can play an important role in raising the child, as does the mother's entire clan. In many gynocratic nations, a primary relationship in the child's life will be with the mother's brother. See page 98 of Mann's *Iroquoian Women: The Gantowisas* for a discussion on the sister-brother and child-Uncle relationships. The role of Uncle serves as a steadfast male relationship in a child's life that cannot be interrupted by divorce and the subsequent loss of the father due to his moving back home to his mother's clan.

Sexuality and Pregnancy

Beliefs about sexuality and pregnancy are deeply influenced by the practice of matrilineal descent in a gynocratic social system. In some of these systems, young people are encouraged to engage in sex when interested in doing so and multiple partners are the norm. Not only does sexual activity denote a step toward adulthood, but it can also develop maturity in the young as they engage in an emotionally and physically powerful adult experience. Young women were expected to control their reproduction by knowing the cycles of their bodies and through herbal medicines to prevent pregnancy. However, since lineage is determined by the mother's clan, a pregnancy is a welcome event and, though children are encouraged to know their father, the matter of paternity bears no consequence for the young woman.

In western culture even unto today, young women becoming pregnant during their teenage years or out of wedlock are often disenfranchised by their family and religious group, socially ostracized, and relatively doomed economically. The issue of determining who is the father of the child is paramount, for this is who will be held responsible for either marrying the young woman or providing court-ordered child support for the first eighteen years of the child's life. Social and welfare workers strongly encourage young women to list the father of the child's name on the child's birth certificate. The term "shotgun wedding" is based on this social theory and practice: A male who impregnates a female in western culture was, in days past at least, held accountable at gunpoint by the expectation that he must marry the woman in order to make her child legitimate. Legitimacy of a human life in the western model is determined by male recognition of a child. More so in decades past but still continued today, all property owned and controlled by a man is passed from him to his eldest male child often skipping daughters and even wives, hence the necessity of being certain about parentage.

Sexually, under the patriarchal model, men knowing as certain as they can that they are the biological father of a child is necessary because of male economic lineage. This requires any woman of western culture to not have sex at all until she is married, thus assuring her first child will indeed be the biological offspring of the husband. This type of economic and political lineage is built into the monotheistic religions of western culture that sharply condemn women for their sexuality outside of a single marriage. Indeed, even in matters of rape, women were condemned to possible death in ancient times and even today in some societies. Controlling women's sexuality means the husband can be certain his property is going to a biological heir, rather than another man's child. This is one way the patriarchal structure is maintained and controlled: through the control of women's sexuality and reproduction. Of course, these controls are absent in the gynocratic structure because lineage is through the mother and all of her social and political status, and rights are passed from her clan to her children. In matrilineal structures, illegitimacy of a child is a stunning and unheard of concept!

Control of Reproduction

Native women practiced control of their reproduction via birth control and abortion because women bear the responsibility for the perpetuation of their nations, and overpopulation is a serious concern. Providing for every person within her clan and ultimately within the nation, which often included tens of thousands of people, was the concern of every clan mother in the Eastern Woodlands and within many other indigenous nations. Excessive reproduction put an extreme burden on the resources of the land of the people. Iroquoian women had only one to two children ideally, as raising a child takes exorbitant amounts of energy from the mother and her entire clan, and a human child requires this type of time, energy, and attention in order to develop into a healthy adult.

Clan Mother

A Clan Mother among the nations of the Eastern Woodlands is a woman who has been elected by her clan members to represent them in the women's council. The term denotes a political office and is a title. It distinguishes a woman member of a clan from the other members because she now will bring their concerns and speak for them in a sociopolitical context. Clan Mothers are political agents and are responsible for the appointment (and if necessary the disbarment) of male sachems and war chiefs, for decisions to maintain peace or call for war, for ensuring the economic sustenance of the people, and for all matters that concern the nation. The head of the women's council was called the Jigonsaseh. This too is a title and a prestigious office. The Jigonsaseh, much like the Beloved Woman of the Cherokee nation, had considerable power in her nation. Professors and students will read about both of these offices in the required texts for the course.

The term *Clan Mother* must not be paralleled with the term used by the Girl and Boy Scouts of America: den mother. A den mother is a woman (usually one of the children's mothers, but not always) who has volunteered her time to lead young girls and boys (separately) in activities that usually involve outdoor skills such as camping. The den mothers also are to instill appropriate values, social skills, and work ethics into the children. This effort is certainly a worthy and important endeavor in our society. However, the den mother and the Native American Clan Mother are two entirely different roles. A Native Clan Mother holds an elected political office and is the voice of political power in her nation, a decision maker of national and international proportions. Her influence reaches out to every corner of her nation. On the other hand, a den mother is a woman volunteer who generously gives her time to young people. She certainly has influence over her young scouts; however, her influence is not a source of national political leadership. A Native American Clan Mother is like a senator; the only difference is that there is no president to appeal to for decisions. In the Iroquois nation, the decisions are made by the women's council of elected Clan Mothers balanced by the men's council and chiefs whom the Clan Mothers appoint.

Koskalaka and Winkte

Terminologies such as gay, lesbian, homosexual, transgendered, bisexual, queer, and gender have meaning in western culture. In indigenous cultures, there are also many, many terms describing human sexual and gender orientation. A key way to understand the Native use of these terms is not through biology, but by spirituality and roles in the nation. Most importantly, those Native terms for nonheterosexual orientation were not negative ones. A person's sexual orientation was considered to be between the individual and the spirits, and therefore anyone else's judgments were inappropriate and not in keeping with cultural beliefs (which valued internal guidance, not external pressures). Judgments in western culture often reflect one's perceptions about the social or religious conformity of another. In Native nations, the only external pressure to conform to was the expectation that people maintained their duties to the nation (work and social roles) and did not infringe upon the rights of another. This concept is clearly outlined in the Iroquois Great Law of Peace.

The term *Twin-spirited*, though often used even by some Native academics to describe homosexual Native peoples, is incorrect in light of Eastern Woodlands culture. It is understood by Eastern Woodlanders that all people are twin-spirited (one earth and one sky spirit), not just homosexuals. Berdache is also incorrect, and is not even a Native word, though it was used by ethnographers to describe Native homosexual behavior.

In many Native nations, homosexuals play important ceremonial roles, can be medicine people, and are honored. Despite hundreds of years of colonization, many ancient traditional stories exist demonstrating the important roles homosexual people played in their nation. However, frequently they played no particularly special roles at all. For example, if a family of all girls needed a son to hunt for them, one of the girls would be made a son and this new son could take a wife for his partner. The important point to remember is that there were no exact prescriptions for identity or roles in most indigenous nations. There were norms, but stepping outside of the norms in relation to sexual and gender identity did not make those individuals a marginalized Other. The obvious reason for this not occurring is because Native nations are communal people: The community is central, not the individual. Therefore, individual choice may be important for the individual, but all individuals were part of the whole and not perceived as outsiders. Indeed, to be perceived as an outsider, on the margin, or as an other, could only happen if a person deliberately left the nation by becoming a citizen of another nation.

Much like Adrienne Rich's classic theory called the Lesbian Continuum—a theory that demonstrates how women in western culture who centralize other women can be called lesbian, not solely those women who have sexual relationships with other women—most Native American cultures centralize women in similar ways. Perhaps in addition to that concept should be added the notion of a Gay Continuum—a theory that men who centralize other men in their lives, but who do not necessarily have a sexual relationship with them, can be called Gay. Certainly, most all Native men centralized each other in all functions of living: from same-sex governing councils to ceremonies to daily work to oral traditions, men kept men's rituals and centralized men and the rising male generations. However, calling all Native women lesbians and all Native men gay would be ridiculous because those terms (lesbian and gay) have western cultural connotations and purposes. Indeed, women who centralize each other were and still are labeled negatively because they are perceived by western culture by their very action to be antithetical to women who centralize men (the cultural ideal). This western idea has no application in indigenous nations.

Most all Native women and men across the nations centralized their same gender, while including homosexual and transgendered peoples, and there was no necessity of creating demeaning labels for women and men who did so (like calling heterosexual women who live in women's community lesbians). Native women and men did not understand themselves to be in conflict based in gender. Women were not expected to centralize men, but they were indeed expected to centralize each other, just as the men were expected to do (centralize each other). Therefore, the necessity of making women and men who centralize their same gender "Others" did not occur because traditionally all Native women and men centralized their same gender in much of their daily activities (same gendered councils, ceremonies, speaking protocols, Keepings, and work activities).

In order to understand homosexuals in a Native cultural context, it is important to remember that personal choice, within the ethics of centralizing the community, was at the core of most Native cultures. Therefore, individuals who understood themselves to not be heterosexually oriented, permanently or occasionally, were not ostracized because casting out people based on their personal choices would be contradictory to communal ethics. Honor toward self and others, upholding the principles of communal ethics toward the entire biosphere, seeking spiritual guidance and insight, and doing one's fair share of the work were the hallmarks of most Native nations. Sexual orientation does not influence any of those duties because heterosexuality was not compulsory nor was the creation of a nuclear family.

One Good Mind

The Iroquois Thanksgiving Address, or speaking from the principle of One Good Mind, demonstrates fundamental beliefs about many Native nations, particularly communal ethics. Understanding this concept is a way to understand communal ethics and the unequivocal inclusion of women in all ceremonial, judicial, and political events. Because both women's and men's councils had speakers, those councils needed both women and men speakers due to same-gendered social protocols to communicate between councils and to other nations. This practice is elaborated upon on page 166 of Mann's *Iroquoian Women: The Gantowisas*.

When a speaker speaks from One Good Mind, she or he has the ability to call upon all the living entities of the universe and allows them to speak through her or him. This occurred before council meetings and during any decision-making process was brought before the councils (166). The practice is a way of gaining communal consensus, not simply human consensus. Entities that speak through the speaker include the sacred cardinal directions, ancestor spirits, and the spirits of all living things, including the wind, rivers, and Mother Earth herself (166). Gaining spiritual acumen and becoming a powerful speaker is a skill a speaker develops, and the speaker is often chosen because of this highly developed ability (166).

What the practice of One Good Mind demonstrates is how the people of the Eastern Woodlands value and are in communion with the whole of the biosphere. Not all Native nations used this practice and certainly did not call it by the Iroquois name. However, allowing the spirits of the whole of life to speak through a medicine person, shaman, leader, or speaker was certainly a common practice among most Native nations, although the practices themselves vary widely. For westerners to comprehend this practice, they must transcend the belief that human life is the most important source for decision making on earth and that the non-human beings on this planet also have spirit and advice to give.

Third, westerners must accept that this is a cultural practice that recognizes the consciousness of other beings, not a Native person's overactive imagination or invented cultural theatrics. Native women had as much, if not more, of a role in this practice as men, as their voice was the voice of the nation's political body.

Classroom Activities

A few questions instructors may wish to pose to the class follow. First, perhaps discuss the prevalence in our contemporary western culture to restrict women's sexuality and not men's. Ask about condemning names invented for men who have multiple heterosexual partners. What about praiseworthy names for men who have multiple partners? Are there praiseworthy names for women who have multiple partners? Next, perhaps open discussion about the condemnation of teenaged girls' sexuality by name-calling and social rejection; how common is the practice? Popular today are "purity balls" where young women declare they will remain asexual until they are married. What are the purposes of this announcement? How then do students understand or make sense of our society's practice to restrict young women's, even married women's, access to birth control and abortion in the presence of cultural practices that condemn women's pregnancy whenever the pregnancy is deemed inappropriate?

Another classroom activity teachers may wish to use is to have students make a list of words denoting that a person of western culture is homosexual, then have them use course materials and lectures to make a list of Native American terms for homosexuals. Next, have them discuss the meanings of the terms and the positive or negative connotative meanings they hold.

Conclusion

As one moves from discipline to discipline, naturally the terminology, concepts, and theories vary. This dynamic is even more pronounced when one moves from culture to culture, as cultures have ancient roots in the conceptualization of the universe, of human behavior, and ways to understand events based specifically in that culture. When teaching a course in Native American Women's Studies, it is essential to use the terms and concepts appropriate to Native cultures in order to not create an ethnocentric perspective about Native practices and beliefs.

CHAPTER V

Patriarchy, Colonial History, and the Waves of Feminism

How the patriarchal structure of western culture began and evolved is important to understand in order to comprehend the complexities of colonization and its impact on Native American people, especially Native women. The culturally complex history of patriarchy, though at its inception had no bearing on indigenous nations in North America, eventually would come to this land and have profoundly devastating consequences for indigenous women. Therefore, looking at the creation and evolution of patriarchy, colonialism, and the waves of feminism offers a window to understand the depth of the consequences Native women, and all Native people, have had to bear and the radical differences between the western and indigenous culture groups.

Patriarchy

Patriarchy is a human-created system that centralizes men, privileging them economically, educationally, socially, spiritually, and physiologically. Men's experiences tend to be universalized in this system, and academic, biological, philosophical, and theological theories and practices are invented and disseminated to further instill in the general population the centrality of men and men's perceptions about life. Social policies, institutions, and laws are created to support these perceptions and to disenfranchise and subordinate women in order to maintain men's privilege. The last two points are important to note: patriarchy is not simply the centralization of men but the simultaneous subjugation of women in order for the men to maintain that privilege for themselves and all subsequent male generations. Patriarchy features an exclusive class system where only a small percentage of males at the top of the system have wealth; however, all males benefit from the patriarchal system because of the inherent privilege of men, even if they are poor. For example, men have held primarily all positions of social power (like judges, professors, lawmakers, United States presidents) only until recently. Therefore, despite any man's socioeconomic class in more contemporary times, he has the system-endorsed "right" to dominate women. These are some components of a patriarchal system. This reality is the ethos (or is it pathos?) of western culture, even in all its varying governing systems over the past several thousand years, and this philosophy remains present in the United States' systems today.

There are many historians who have written about the possible beginnings and evolution of patriarchy. There are multiple accepted theories on these origins. One theorist is Gerda Lerner and in her groundbreaking book, titled *The Creation of Patriarchy* (1986), she notes that the process of class formation in Mesopotamian society several thousand years before the Common Era (B.C.E.) "incorporated an already pre-existing condition of male dominance over women" (200). She then adds that it was the later development of a monotheistic religion that fully institutionalized the exclusion of women (200). Separate from religious theology and writing, Greek historical scholarship developed in the sixth and fifth centuries B.C.E., "but the construct of history was a male product and would so remain for another 2500 years" (201). Lerner notes that in the seventh century B.C.E. Hesiod "achieves what Hebrew myth achieved in the story of the Fall—he places the blame on woman and her sexual nature for bringing evil into the world" (204). Much as I am calling for more routine inclusion of courses in Native American ancient women's traditions, more routine inclusion of woman-centered, pre-patriarchal cultures from the Mesopotamian geographic area in academia would also be enlightening and empowering for students.

Lerner states unequivocally that "as was the case in Mesopotamia and Israel, Greece of the eighth through the fifth century B.C. was a class society with slavery, and it was a thoroughly patriarchal society...the fact of women's legal and social subordination is undisputed" (202). She notes that Aristotle claims "the male is by nature superior, and the female inferior; and the one rules and the other is ruled" (208) thereby justifying "class dominance logically from his gender definitions" (209).

From the Spartan citizen soldier to secular Greek philosophy to the earliest monotheistic doctrines, women of western culture have been barred from direct positions of power in every arena of human social systems. The reasoning for this lack of representation stems from male claims that women are inferior intellectually, physically, and spiritually, and that the male philosophers and later the monotheistic male God ordains it to be so. This information was written on paper and transmitted from generation to generation of males and thereby became institutionalized: a knowledge base that was universalized and practiced for thousands of years. Women were barred from most formal education since the beginning of western culture until around the beginning of the twentieth century. Women's inferiority within western culture became what we refer to as common knowledge, a given, something everyone understands to be true. This patriarchal theoretical framework—with its origins in the nuclear family structure in antiquity—then got translated to the state, as Lerner argues. The state is the political structure of the nation, which has economic implications of course. This structure was kept in place, despite wars and varying political structures, over thousands of years and was then brought to North America with the European settlers.

Lerner notes that "in every known society it was women of conquered tribes who were first enslaved, whereas men were killed" (213). She uses this fact to support her theory that this practice was what created sex and race oppression in class structures. Further, she notes that another cause of oppression was because "the first gender-defined social role for women was to be those who were exchanged in marriage transactions" (214). These practices reinforced women's oppression and exploitation, and the practices then became evidence that supported the whole society's belief in women's inferiority to men. Lerner also notes that "class for men was and is based on their relationship to the means of production: those who owned the means of production could dominate those who did not" (215).

Lerner's observations are appropriate for the history of non-indigenous cultures in the geographic areas that spawned patriarchy. There are also many other theories within academia about the creation of patriarchy. However, they have no bearing on the indigenous cultures throughout North America (and most likely throughout the world), particularly in the Eastern Woodlands.

To illustrate, I will respond to Lerner's theoretical observations. In the Eastern Woodlands, both Native women and men were captured during war raids and members of both genders had the opportunity for advancement to full citizenship in the nation if they chose to do so. One popular example of this practice is evidenced with the famous historic settler captive Mary Jemison who became a notable Seneca clan mother. Second, captive women were not raped by Native men, as this practice was not at all part of the Native culture. Rape, or exerting one's power and will over another (almost always man to woman or child), was a heinous act to Native people and a certain abhorred and feared mixing of sky and earth medicine, sure to have a dangerous outcome for the man! Therefore, sexual oppression was another practice not present in gynocratic indigenous nations. In addition to the problems with Lerner's captive theory is the historic fact about Native Americans of the Eastern Woodlands and many other nations that it was women, and women alone (clan mothers on the women's council), who made decisions about all war captives, not men. Women, children, elders, and the mentally and physically impaired were legally considered Innocents. This legal status protected them from harm during times of war. Restitution to a clan for the intentional or accidental death of a woman was twice that of restitution for a man. This was not because of the loss of a bio-

was maintained by most nations prevented any type of gender-based dominance from occurring. Dominance by any gender would be understood as an out-of-balance scenario and, therefore, dangerous to the life of the nation's social structure.

Though historians and anthropologists often attempt to parallel the public/private sphere gender framework concept onto gynocratic indigenous cultures, it does not apply. Indeed, many feminist historians and anthropologists understand the concept of the gender-based public/private sphere split in western cultural systems as an invention of industrial patriarchy and thus reject the notion. The concept does not apply to most Native nations and here is why: any socioeconomic system in a patriarchal structure favors men despite their need for women's private sphere production of goods and services. Men and their work are made central in such a system, even if women are also producers. Further, women themselves are made commodities: if they, and therefore their work, are absent for whatever reason (like death) from the private sphere (the home), men could/and still can easily find another woman to replace her. According to some theorists, women during the colonial period are not understood to be powerless because they had so-called "private sphere" power. From an indigenous cultural perspective, settler women during the colonial period may have had some value within the home, but it mattered little since they were barred from what Native people consider basic human rights. Claiming that any gender-based means of production within a patriarchal system is gender complementary must be defined in wholly separate ways from what that term means in an indigenous gynocratic context. They are radically different, and readings from the required text list in chapter two will clarify this point.

The history of many Native cultures in light of Lerner's important observations about the history and machinations of patriarchy only further supports and reveals the presence of Native women's power in their nations and the social constructs that created that power. Examination of other theorists' work would also be enlightening. In some Native traditional nations, the presence of the patriarchal practices that Lerner and others note *are* present in the social structures, yet they are expressed and conceptualized differently. This would be an interesting research topic for students and is offered in the Research Topics list in chapter two.

Colonial History

The patriarchal socioeconomic structure just discussed was the very foundation present in the systems brought to North America with the first European settlers. Though there were certainly variances from the structures present in Europe at the time, the same beliefs were in place about social status, power, and economic control based in gender. What the earliest settlers—both clergy and lay folk alike—saw in the structures of Native nations in the East astounded them: The Native women held leadership roles! From the journals of the earliest (1500s) Jesuit and Franciscan priests to settler leaders like Benjamin Franklin and George Washington to the earliest suffragists like Mathilda Jocelyn Gage, the EuroAmericans were shocked, outraged, or inspired by the gynocratic systems before them. Mann quotes Father Lafitau's words written in 1724 about the Iroquois: "Nothing is more real, however, than the women's superiority. It is they who really maintain the tribe...In them resides all the real authority...they are the soul of the councils, the arbiters of peace and war...(*Iroquoian Women* 182). What is little known today about Native gynocracies, and even outright denied by some academics, was common knowledge during colonial times. Evidence of this common knowledge is clearly demonstrated in the earliest primary sources: journals of priests, journals and public policies of United States' presidents, ethnographers, and suffragists. Aside from the suffragists, the males wrote extensively about the Native women's power and how deeply troubled the settler men felt about that fact.

Aside from the land-grabbing motivation behind the new American government's policies, a primary purpose for the mass murder and relocation of Native peoples was to destroy the Native gynocratic systems. Destruction of this system was important for two reasons: settler men did not want the settler women to gain the type of power Native women had; and destruction of the Native women's power meant the destruction of the indigenous cultures, which was necessary for total colonization of the Native people. The earliest settler men and priests coming to North America knew all too well about the gynocracies of the Native Americans and set out to destroy them in order to complete their task of colonization, which meant total control of the land and her people. A primary tool they used to do this was the earliest doctrines of western culture that support the subservience and oppression of women: monotheistic religious texts.

The lives of colonial EuroAmerican women during the takeover of North America from the Native peoples were quite grim. They were veritable slaves in their own homes and had no legal rights that protected them from their husbands or the state. In another book by Gerda Lerner, *The Woman in American History* (1971), she chronicles the history of colonial women. Lerner writes at length about EuroAmerican women's plight and notes that they were subservient to their husbands; subject to public punishment for "speaking against" their husband; domestic slaves; unable to own land; unable to vote; unable to inherit property or money if there was a male heir; played no role in governance; were sexually diminished through prostitution and so on (12–24).

Two common colonial practices that were perpetrated upon wives by their husbands to publicly humiliate them for not obeying were punishments called bridling and dunking. Bridling was a literal leather bridle (like a horse's bridle) that was placed around a woman's head to restrict her mouth and therefore her speech. At times, there were metal barbs attached to this that stuck into the woman's mouth and gums causing excruciating pain. Dunking was done in public to a woman as she sat tied to a seat (like a see-saw) and was lowered into a body of water upon the orders of her husband. Both of these practices were aimed at silencing colonial women and demonstrated the uncontrolled power of men over women.

In relation to colonial women's legal rights, Lerner notes:

> The husband was the sole guardian over the children, even in case of divorce. He could dispose of his wife's earnings at will and squander her inherited property. His authority over the home was absolute, and wife and children were without protection if he abused his power. Divorces were seldom granted. (14)

She continues to explain in this passage that colonial newspapers were filled with advertisements taken out by husbands looking for their runaway wives because running away was one of the few recourses a woman had to escape her plight.

Considering the events of the colonial era and the lives of EuroAmerican women, it is no wonder settler men were alarmed by the Native gynocracies in the East and sought to destroy them. Risking the empowerment of settler women would mean a shift in the power base of the new American government and social structure, a risk they did not wish to take. Deliberate destruction of the Native women's wampum belts (these were the records of lineage chiefs, council meeting minutes, names, and so on) was a military strategy enacted during the American Revolutionary War era by George Washington. The purpose was to erode Native women's source of power and the records of that power in order to permanently skew the historic record, an action that has been quite successful until recently. See chapter four of *Land of the Three Miamis* titled "He Burns It," page 81, and for a definitive study about George Washington's role in colonization I recommend Mann's book *George Washington's War on Native America* (2005).

Despite the concerted political and military efforts of male colonial leaders to destroy the matrilineal indigenous systems, there were other settlers who were paying attention to the Native gynocracies: the EuroAmerican women. The suffragist movement, or First Wave Feminist movement, begun in the late 1700s, was inspired by the Iroquois clan mothers themselves. Mary Wollstonecraft's famous work *The Vindication of the Rights of Woman* (1792) was crafted after her partner returned from the new America filled with stories about the rights of Native women. Mathilda Jocelyn Gage was a radical woman writer on the scene during the First Wave as well, and she was adopted into the Mohawk nation by the clan mothers and took her lessons from them. The famous Seneca Falls Convention (1848) was held in the heart of the Iroquois nation's lands, home of the clan mothers' power. See the two books in the bibliography in chapter two by Sally Roesch Wagner that offer a detailed history and literary connections from Native women to earliest suffragists and First Wave feminism from this period.

The Native American gynocratic structures were the foundation of inspiration for the colonial women in North America who had to endure all manner of daily humiliation and could not be the center of their own life. Imagine how they must have felt and what their thoughts might have been as they ventured away from a home where they were the servant without rights and any recourse to be protected from abuse, no control over their reproduction or protection from rape, and no legal rights to educate themselves, vote, or own property—and then they witnessed Native women not only governing themselves, but their people. The shock of it was tremendous and empowering. Many settler women captives of Native nations did not wish to return to their settler family and community when they were found by settler militia. Mary Jemison was only one of many women who did not wish to return to her family and people after enjoying the privilege and power of being a woman in a Native nation.

The Waves of Feminism

The eras of historic social changes, activism, organizing, and scholarship created by feminist writers and scholars are called waves. First Wave feminism is the era referring to the earliest suffragists' movement engineered by women like Elizabeth Cady Stanton

(1815–1902) and Susan B. Anthony (1820–1906). In the previous paragraphs, I have mentioned briefly the connection between some of these feminists and Native cultural thought and practice. The First Wave era include women gaining the right to vote (1920) and women's increased public presence. Important to note is that the waves terminology is at times criticized by feminist scholars because it tends to focus on the achievements and events around only Anglo women in the United States and Europe, thereby ignoring the myriad achievements and events of women from other ethnicities and races throughout the world.

The Second Wave of feminism in the United States began in the 1960s and is often referred to as the "personal is political era" or "add women and stir" era. This was the era of the women's liberation movement and involved direct political action that was often connected to the Civil Rights era thinking also occurring at this time. The scholarship created during the 1960s and 1970s by feminist scholars like Gerda Lerner, Dorothy E. Smith, Rayna Rapp, Evelyn Fox Keller, Nancy Shrom Dye, Shalumit Reinharz, Rayna Green, and many other social scientists, historians, activists, and anthropologists set the stage for revealing the problems of women's oppression and solutions to creating equality. They wished to add women to the historic record and to the living culture of their times: a culture that still barred women from most positions of power and that continued to erase women's historic, artistic, and social contributions to humanity. In this section, I will look at some of the observations these scholars made about women in western culture, and then I will discuss them from a Native cultural perspective.

Another important contribution by Gerda Lerner was a book she edited titled *The Female Experience: An American Documentary* (1977). In the book's introduction Lerner asserts that "the emergence of feminist consciousness as a historical phenomenon is an essential part of the history of women" (xxxiv). The book is organized by topics, such as "The Female Life Cycle: Childhood, Marriage, Motherhood, and the Single State," "Just a Housewife," and "Old Age, Sickness, and Death." These topics alone are revealing about the roles of women in western culture and deserve to be addressed from a Native perspective.

The Native Female Traditional Life Cycle might entail the following: Childhood among the Clan Family; Moontime Ceremony; Sexual Expression; Marriage, Divorce and Child Rearing; Communal Education; Clan and National Citizenship; Leadership and Governing; Spiritual Wisdom; Grandmother/Elder Roles; Maintaining the Basket for the Rising Generations. These signposts in a Native woman's traditional life (of course they would vary widely from nation to nation) demonstrate that her life is centered on her own experiences, her own body, her own connections and support of her nation, and her own contribution to the next generations of her nation. To Native women of the Eastern Woodlands and many other gynocratic Native nations, marriage and motherhood are only two of the many significant purposes or experiences of her life. They are not the sole and primary definers of her identity, which would indicate that mandatory heterosexuality within a singular, monogamous relationship and the expectation of biological reproduction were not narrow expectations of every Native woman. Divorce was common in the Eastern Woodlands, just as the expectation of personally developing spiritual acumen, leadership, community service and cooperation, and whatever talents she possessed were common. These are important distinctions between the life cycles of a woman from a Native culture versus a woman from western culture. Of course, I must emphasize, that there are many further distinctions among Native nations themselves. The essential point to recognize is that there are wide differences between perceptions and practices of a woman's life cycle in a patriarchal structure versus a matrilineal one.

Next, the anthology *The Prism of Sex: Essays in the Sociology of Knowledge* by Julia A. Sherman and Evelyn Torton Beck (1979) characterizes Second Wave feminism because the essays discuss the absence and reasons for the absence of women "from creative intellectual work" (6). The editors note that "women in the scholarly world do not see as women, but as men have taught them to see—through the prism of the male sex" (5). They point out that, at the time, only tenured and tenure-track professors were permitted to give papers at most academic conferences, and women rarely held these positions, thus omitting them from participation in a scholarly setting where their intellectual ideas and perspectives could be heard.

An essay from the anthology that is particularly interesting because it discusses issues with gender and the reporting and conceptualization of history is Nancy Shrom Dye's work "Clio's American Daughters: Male History, Female Reality." She explores why American women were/are excluded from history: women's work is insignificant to men, and not included in historic works because men write the history (11). She notes that "women have maintained a distinct female culture" but that this culture is hidden from men because it is a private culture (11). Dye discusses the "doctrine of spheres": men are public and women are private; men are producers and women are consumers, but notes that by 1870 this notion was disintegrating because women were out in women's clubs (14).

Dye asserts that women are not in the western cultural historical narrative because male historians are unable to understand the realities of women's lives and this has distorted history up to present times (22). She continues to recognize that the periodization of western history is sexist because it is irrelevant to women's history as it does not reflect significant changes in women's lives (22). She calls for a women's chronology of history that would force the acceptance that women's reality is different from men's (22).

Dye's essay raises fascinating issues when comparing Native culture with western culture in relation to gender experience. The doctrine of spheres she discusses seems to be, at first glance, exactly the same as the Native model: Native women in the Eastern Woodlands ran the local government and the home (private) and Native men controlled forest management and were chiefs, soldiers, and diplomats (public). However, that would be looking at Natives through the prism of western culture, to borrow her example. What the Native cultural model actually denotes are not gender prescriptions for social functioning, but a deliberate cosmic/spiritual-oriented social construction for the balance of the nation. The Native gynocratic model does not generally disenfranchise or subordinate those who are in the so-called private sphere (the women) and elevate or privilege those who are in the so-called public sphere (men). This is certainly true in the case of the Iroquois. The public/private sphere model is a system of power that privileges the producers (men) and disenfranchises the consumers (women) because that model is based on an economic system that centralizes capitalism or personal gain—a model that generally did not exist in gynocratic Native cultures. Both Native women and men in gender balanced nations were producers; indeed, women were the sole distributors of production from the land and had significant economic power in the Eastern Woodlands. Herein is another area where Dye's salient points about American women do not apply to most Native culture systems.

Dye's point that American women are omitted from their nation's historic record, but that they, nevertheless, have their own history to report is relevant to the gendered practices of many Native nations. From a Native perspective, what Dye is arguing for is gendered Keepings and gendered protocols for reporting those Keepings—two ancient practices of the Eastern Woodlands. Indeed, Native men would, and do, have difficulty reporting the history and traditions of women—most of which are kept from them because they are not women and do not and should not have access to that knowledge. The same rule applies to women in relation to men's keepings—those are the purview of the men.

However, where this fits with Dye's point about the presence of gendered historical experiences, it fails when applied more broadly. For example, as Dye notes, American women's historic experiences and culture are distinct from men's and are absent from the American historic record—as a point of national record, women's historic experiences are not routinely repeated orally, written about in textbooks, or taught in schools as part of the whole American historic experience. However, in the Native historic record, women were traditionally as much a part of the history as were the men and this was transmitted in both a closed (by thinking reflects Freud's theory of "rationality over personal experience" that only further alienates and marginalizes women from themselves (144). Here again gendered experience holds values in the culture: men's way of speaking and their culture are valued, whereas women's way is devalued. Smith continues by saying that men or the dominant class has taken over women's thinking, language, conditions, fantasies, dreams, and so on, so that she no longer knows herself beyond the male definition (144). This scenario is reinforced through doctors, historians, psychologists, and literature, all of whom continue to separate women from their own lives and prevent them from developing a woman-defined self (144).

Smith also notes that the female norm as defined by scholars like Freud (i.e., formerly universally accepted, and ludicrous, Freudian theories such as "male castration" by women and women's "penis envy") was humiliating to women, but when they reacted to this humiliating, subordinate definition of the self, that reaction was labeled as a pathology (136). In other words, when women noted the absurdity of Freud's theories about them, the women were then labeled as sick, which only further condemned them and elevated the male labelers. In terms of feminist theorists like Simone de Beauvoir and Betty Friedan, Smith asserts that de Beauvoir does not conceptualize or challenge the norms of society about women as Friedan does. "The feminist mystiques of society pervaded our identity and created our values, beliefs, morals, and sense of self" is Smith's observation that men's culture erases the very being of women in America (136). Last, she notes that the celebrated writing of authors like D. H. Lawrence "annihilated our sexual self" because male literary works defined femininity and sexuality for women that was destructive, male-centered, and made women appear to be pathological (137).

Smith's points sharply demonstrate the contrast between western and Native culture in relation to gendered experience. All the points she notes above which are present in western culture are absent in many Native cultures. In most nations, women and men both had their own Keepings and traditions that were quite different, but both were equally valued. Native men neither dictated to Native women about their experiences nor defined who they were, and they did not keep stories that delegitimized, slandered, or mocked their experiences. In fact, they did not keep women's stories at all! Women kept their own stories, thereby defining the events and their own identity as they understood it. Most importantly, they took their cues from the ancient traditional stories of their nation, and these stories often centralized and valued women: women's experiences, women's bodily functions, women's national leadership, women's wisdom, and women's power. This is a remarkable difference between the Native and western cultural models and, certainly in the Eastern Woodlands, it is simply anathema to mix earth and sky medicine inappropriately. What this analysis means in traditional terms is that men (sky medicine) must not ever speak of women's (earth medicine) traditions, or literal catastrophe can occur (like a tornado).

To most Native peoples, devaluing one part of the balanced half of the entire social structure would be unbeneficial to everyone—something that is arguably true even for the patriarchal American system. Indeed, there are some Native nations whose very language is gendered—linguistically women have women's words for objects and events and men have men's words for the very same objects and events. Exploring this topic and the linguistic examples further would make a challenging and interesting research assignment for advanced students!

We are currently in the Third Wave of the feminist movement, and many activists of our era are looking back to the community-building agenda of Second Wave feminists to determine how the women's movement might continue. Conflicts arising from this period include the struggles women now face with understanding and living out their feminist identity in contemporary times. Should they be a mother, an executive, or both? How does a woman, or any person, accomplish that? If a woman stays at home to raise a child, is she an antifeminist, a failure of a woman, or a sell-out to patriarchy? If a woman does not have a child and does not marry a man, has she failed as a woman? What is freedom for women and does western women's newfound freedom merely exploit other women from nonindustrialized countries or the poor women of the United States, often women of color? These are some of the deeply conflicted questions primarily mainstream, Anglo-American women ask themselves. The experiences of women across the myriad of American ethnicities vary, of course.

Since the 1980s and 1990s, there has been a backlash occurring against feminists. This backlash is a philosophy that often gets enacted via violence (in language, scholarship, and individual action) that says women are the cause of men's problems and any economic problems within our country occur because of feminist thinking and the "selfish" actions of feminist women. Backlash is hatred of women and woman-centered living, but how is woman-centered living defined anymore? Backlash against women feminists is just another way of centralizing the needs and perceptions of men and the patriarchal system. This strategy too is intended to get the focus off of women's experiences and their oppression in the system and refocus it upon men's experiences and the validation of the system itself.

Again, these questions about women's identity and roles in society were irrelevant in traditional Eastern Native nations, and many other Native nations, because a woman could easily bear and raise a child while performing her civic leadership and economic duties and continue her education. Parenting was easily possible because her clan was ever present to care for her and her child. No choice was necessary. Native women were not economically penalized by default because they had a child (while married or not) because most Native systems were not based in capitalist, but rather in communal ethics. The sometimes devastating choices contemporary American women must make based on childrearing and economics, Native women never had to face. Native women did not have to choose an identity (mother or executive) or forfeit some aspiration because she also wished to have a child. Further, dichotomizing women's experiences into biological roles versus roles traditionally held by men (public sphere with economic power) could not occur in indigenous cultures because the cultures themselves did not use that economic power model. Native women's experiences with power and autonomy within gynocratic nations and in nongynocratic nations varied widely, and each nation must be understood within the context of its cosmology and cultural practices.

Conclusion

In traditional Native cultural perspective, looking at the events and problems of contemporary times demands an analysis of the historic roots of the people. What has happened to women in western culture must be understood in terms of what happened at the beginning of western history and how gender was understood then. Further, significant events in women's historic experience, like the Catholic Church's European witch trials that enforced the torture and murder of at least hundreds of thousands, if not millions, of women, continue to affect contemporary women. To the Native American, there is no disconnection between history and the now. These notions of time are understood to be connected and mutually influential. Therefore, the problems American women face today are directly linked to the historic events of their ancient ancestors and the philosophies and social structures of the times since then. The same is of course true for Native people. At the beginning of time were the Creators—Spider Woman and Sky Woman and many more—and their legacy reaches out to the Native women of today and empowers them. Despite colonization and severe damage to Native traditions, the wisdom and literal presence of these ancient grandmothers are directly linked to the Native women alive today—their granddaughters—and the ancient wisdom of these Grandmother Beings is available to all people on Turtle Island who wish to honor them.

CHAPTER VI

Native American Women Today

Since colonization of North America by Europeans, the lives of Native American people have been drastically and detrimentally altered—permanently. To the Eastern Woodlands indigenous survivors of the events leading up to and culminating in the American Indian Holocaust of 1776 and the Indian Wars west of the Mississippi after the Greenville Treaty was signed at the turn of the eighteenth century, life as a Native American person has been a battle for personal survival, cultural survival, and constant negotiation of identity.

For Native American women, the struggle for survival has specific challenges since the colonizing culture (western culture) brought misogyny with it and all the religious, social, and judicial restraints a woman-persecuting society engenders. Therefore, not only do Native American women have to face the battles any colonized people must meet, but they must fight the beliefs that render them subordinate because they are women. This dynamic runs entirely counter to the historic and cultural beliefs of gynocratic indigenous people, so the blow to the women because of their gender is particularly severe. Once the Native women were leaders, and now they are relegated by their own nations and the larger non-Native nation to second-class citizenship, are targets for interpersonal and sexual violence, and their gynocratic governing structures are called myths by some scholars and Native peoples due to centuries of colonization.

Despite this dismal situation, Native women continue to organize, stay connected with their traditions, speak out, educate themselves about the colonizer's government, fight the United States government and often their own nations, and create art, laws, and a presence that reflects an undeniably Native worldview. They have not only survived but flourished despite the enormous challenges a military occupation of their lands, genocide, and forced assimilation have created.

In this chapter current statistics of the effects of colonization on Native North American women are discussed along with the social and political organizations and art created by Native women. The statistics report suffering, but the organizations demonstrate the cultural resiliency and strength of indigenous women — a legacy that is directly connected to the ancient cultural beliefs of a people who recognize foremost that Beauty and Life Medicine endure, and Ugliness and Death Medicine can only prevail briefly because of their inherent weakness.

Statistics on Violence

What research about Native American women and violence demonstrates from decade to decade is that the incidence of violence against them is disproportionately higher than the number of violent acts against any other group in America. In an April 2007 *New York Times* article titled "For Indian Victims of Sexual Assault, a

Tangled Legal Path," writer Ralph Blumenthal notes that one in three Native American women is raped in her lifetime, which is almost double the national average of 18 percent, according to the United States Justice Department. "In 86 percent of the cases, the perpetrators were non-Native men, while in the population at large, the attacker and victim are usually from the same ethnic group" (Blumenthal). What this means is that indigenous women are targeted for sexual violence by men, primarily EuroAmerican, who are not Native. Native women are perceived by non-Native men as objects for perpetrating acts of hatred and sexual violence in order to humiliate them. As domestic violence and sexual assault agencies throughout the United States teach our communities, all violence is about power and control of one person over another, and rape is not for a man's sexual gratification, but for power over a woman or child. This is a direct effect of colonization. Native people are still perceived as subhuman, as they were portrayed in ethnographic and religious literature and political writing during the earliest European settler contact with them, and this portrayal has not ended today as these same texts are routinely taught in academia and representations of indigenous peoples as un-Godly savages is reinforced via sports mascots and movies. The *New York Times* article reports a particular incident when a young Native woman was gang raped by three white men who held her prisoner for three days, burned her with cigarettes, and obviously terrorized her. When she reported the incident to the police, they dismissed the attack as consensual, even in light of the cigarette burn marks (Blumenthal). This incident is not the exception but the rule when it comes to violence against Native

American women and the judicial system's response to that violence.

There are many organizations to help Native women across the United States to research the problem, support victims, rehabilitate Native perpetrators, and raise awareness about violence against Native women. Some of these organizations include the Office on Violence Against Women, Women Empowering Women for Indian Nations, Sacred Circle of the National Resource Center to End Violence Against Native Women, Safety for Indian Women from Sexual Assault Offenders Demonstration Initiative, Spirits of Hope Coalition, Help in Crisis, and the Native American Legal Resource Center at the Oklahoma City University School of Law, among many others inside and outside of Native communities and reservations.

An essential source for information and networking about the serious challenges facing indigenous women today is INCITE! Women of Color Against Violence, the largest grassroots, multiracial feminist organization in the United States that seeks to empower women to combat violence. *Conquest: Sexual Violence and American Indian Genocide* is the work of Andrea Smith, cofounder of INCITE!; the work is listed in the Recommended Reading list in chapter two.

Leadership

In previous chapters the leadership roles of Native North American women of gynocratic nations are discussed, including the history, official titles, and cultural beliefs about women as leaders in precolonial Native nations. Some of these titles include Jigonsaseh (Iroquois), Beloved Woman (Cherokee), and more broadly Clan

Mother (an elected office present in most Native nations). What office women did not hold in most Native nations was the office of Chief. In the Iroquois nation, the office of Chief was held by a man who was appointed by the women's council and who gained the right to be Chief through the women because specific clans traditionally held the lineage for Chiefs of certain clans. When the Chief died, or was removed because of neglecting his duty, the Clan Mothers appointed someone else. This was their right.

In precolonial times, Native women of the Eastern Woodlands were not chiefs because that was not part of their duty to the nation. Native women ran the local government and had final word over matters of war, peace councils, economic decisions, prisoners of war, and so on. They ran internal affairs and exerted their will over all national matters as well, but from the inside of the nation. It was men who were engaged in matters outside the nation: forest management, diplomacy and gifting, conducting wars as soldiers and generals, and official meetings as Chief. The Speakers for the women's council were present at all events that had bearing on the nation and traveled to councils outside the nation. These Speakers were the voice and ears of the women's council.

Women of the Eastern Woodlands, and in many gynocratic Native nations, held economic control in their nations via their connection with and sole right to distribute the bounty of the land. This right, which came directly from Sky Woman in the Iroquois creation story, gave indigenous women autonomy over their life and power in their nations: economic, political, and social power. The office of Chief would obviously be a lesser office than any office held by the women for the sole fact that it was a man's office and not a woman's office: women held not just significant sway politically, socially, and economically in precolonial Native nations, but they had the final word in all legislative matters. Indeed, balance of earth/sky medicine, of women and men's duties to the nation, was paramount in gynocratic nations, but women certainly held the central role—this was not to the men's detriment, however, as I have already discussed.

In light of this indisputable historic-cultural fact, common perceptions among many Native nations today that Native women were never leaders and should not become leaders are alarming. Colonized thinking and colonized behaviors are at the heart of these perceptions, but it is Native American women who must fight this negative assimilation, and that is precisely what they are doing!

In a February 2006 article in the *New York Times* entitled "As Tribal Leaders, Women Still Fight Old Views," author Monica Davey notes that "in the past quarter-century, the number of women serving as top tribal leaders has nearly doubled...69 of the more than 500 federally recognized American Indian tribes were headed by women." She adds that "by 2006 the number of women leaders of tribes was 133 among more than 560 tribes."

It states in the article that Wilma Mankiller was the first woman elected to office of Principal Chief of the Cherokee Nation of Oklahoma and that she was "the first modern woman to lead a major American Indian tribe" (Davey). Mankiller is quoted in the article as remembering a remark from a Native man during a meeting who said, "If we elect a woman we'll be the laughing stock of all tribes" (Davey). A scholar of American Indian Studies from a South Dakota university attempted to correct the record about Native women leaders by noting that "In some tribes, clan mothers had a direct say in picking leaders, and female tribe members might be medicine women, holy women, or responsible for deciding whether to approve a war" (Davey). Unfortunately, this fact often goes unheeded by some Native people today because of the effects of colonization (cultural erasure) on generations of their people.

Throughout the article, Native women are quoted as saying that because they are leading their nations they are "less traditional" and that women were not typically leaders. Indeed, in some Native nations—nations that were not gynocratic—women did not have the prominent leadership roles they did in women-centered ones. However, the conflict—both internal and external—that Native women leaders experience is due to colonization because Native women in most nations were historically leaders since ancient times. Evidence of this was discussed at length in previous chapters and can be researched by students by reviewing earliest settler contact journals and indigenous traditional stories that have not been colonized (rewritten to reflect Eurocentric cultural perspectives). A discussion of EuroAmerican and Native American primary sources and the myriad of problems surrounding them can be found throughout Barbara Mann's book *Iroquoian Women: The Gantowisas*.

Politically, contemporary Native American women are active in reclaiming power for themselves in order to empower their nations. In recent years, Native women are more involved in leadership positions in Native governments and the United States government. One national organization is the Indigenous Women's Political Caucus, which was formed to protect Native women's sovereignty and other issues; its mission is discussed by

David Melmer in a February 2007 *Indian Country Today* article entitled "Women Set Up Network to Support Their Issues." In the
article former Oglala Sioux Chief Cecelia Fire Thunder and South
Dakota State Senator Theresa Two Bulls discuss issues facing Native women today and the advocacy that is needed for them. Methods to promote their nations' welfare, such as halting liquor
sales on and near reservations, fighting for healthcare for women
and their children, and gaining access to political power, are re-
vealed in the article. The obstacles before them are also made
clear: the colonized thinking of their own people that oppresses
women and perpetuates the entire nation's suffering.

Military participation and leadership of contemporary Native
American women are also a part of the new roles they play. In a
November 2001 *Indian Country Today* article entitled "Honor the
Women Who Served," writer Brenda Finnicum offers a condensed
history of the Native women who participated in United States
military and nursing care from the Spanish American War to the
War in Iraq. She notes that Native American women since the
Spanish American War "were starting a tradition of service in the
[United States] military" (Finnicum). She notes that Native wom-
en were officers and enlisted personnel in the military, were pilots
in the Air Force, and also served in the Red Cross and the Navy
and Army Nurse Corps overseas and on hospital ships (Finnicum). They served in Desert Shield/Storm operations, and one of
the American servicewoman casualties of the Iraq War was Army
Pfc. Lori Piestewa (Hopi).

What Finnicum's article fails to note is the much more important traditional roles of indigenous women from precolonial and
colonial times as war generals, soldiers, and military spies for

their people. From the Jigonsaseh's (Seneca) Corn Way Revolution from 800 C.E. to Pocahontas' (Potawatomi) work as a spy to Tekonwatonti's (Mohawk) pivotal role in the American Revolutionary War as a feared (by the British) military leader, Native American women have been fighting for the life and causes of their people whenever it was necessary. The essential observation in these historic facts is that Native women were leaders in their own right, and these roles were often available to them in their traditional nations. Being a tribal or national leader should not be considered untraditional by contemporary Native American women, but should be seen for what it is: a continuation of the legacy that began with Sky Woman and Spider Woman, was expressed in the offices of Jigonsaseh and Beloved Woman, and is expressed today in the tenacious activism of Native American women who have transcended the colonized identities forced upon them and their people for centuries. Even in traditionally nongynocratic Native nations, the presence of women creators and their legacy of power is present—despite it being subverted by their nation's sociopolitical structures and practices.

An important source for news and information about indigenous women is the Indigenous Women's Network. Their website (www.indigenouswomen.org) notes that they are a grassroots organization established in 1985 by indigenous women that supports future generations of indigenous women by passing traditional knowledge to them. The organization offers a worldwide network of support to Native women on issues ranging from healthcare to protecting the earth to rallying for legislation that supports their causes.

Arts

Contemporary Native American women are flourishing in the many genres of artistic expression available to them within the new colonial nation in which they now find themselves. From directing films, writing literature, performing concerts, and writing operas to engaging in traditional arts like making pottery and weaving baskets and blankets, Native American women are present in the artistic world of America. Much of their work is showcased in not only local museums but in the Smithsonian National Museum of the American Indian in Washington, D.C.

In a May 2005 article from *Indian Country Today* entitled "Daughters from the Stars," the longest-running women's theater company in North America is discussed. "Spiderwoman Theater takes its name from the Hopi's Spider Woman, who created people and taught them to weave" the caption explains.

The Indigenous Women Filmmakers Network is another organization that supports Native women. Some members of the network have received major awards. Alanis Obomsawin is one of Canada's most distinguished documentary filmmakers. She has made over thirty documentaries on issues affecting First Nations peoples and retrospectives of her films have appeared at New York's Museum of Modern Art and Boston's Museum of Fine Arts.

Wordcraft Circle of Native Writers is an organization that supports Native artistic expression and has awarded many contemporary Native women writers for their work.

Singer/songwriters like Ulali, Buffy St. Marie, and Joanne Shenandoah are nationally recognized recording artists and have won major awards (including a Grammy in some instances) for their work.

What these brief accolades of Native women artists denote is that Native women are not only surviving the effects of colonization, but they are turning devastation into life. They are taking the colonizer's tools—language (English and Spanish) and methods of transmission (film, paper and ink, recording devices)—and using them to perpetuate their culture and the life of their nations. More precisely, the cultural values of Native Americans are far from dead or lost, but are being expressed, every day, in the broader world culture as truly as they ever were.

Works Cited

Blumenthal, Ralph. "For Indian Victims of Sexual Assault, a Tangled Legal Path." *New York Times* 25 April 2007. 23 Oct. 2007 <*http://www.nytimes.com/2007/04/25/us/25rape.html*>.

"Daughters from the Stars." *Indian Country Today* 18 May 2005, A1.

Davey, Monica. "As Tribal Leaders, Women Still Fight Old Views." *New York Times* 4 Feb. 2006. 23 Oct 2007 <*http://www.nytimes.com/2006/02/04/national/04tribe.html*>.

Finnicum, Brenda. "Honor the women Who Served." *Indian Country Today* 13 Nov. 2001. 23 Oct 2007 <*http://www.indiancountrytoday.com/content/.cfm?id=2823.html*>.

Lerner, Gerda. *The Creation of Patriarchy*. New York: Oxford University Press, 1986.

———. *The Female Experience: An American Documentary*. Indianapolis: Bobbs-Merrill, 1977.

———. *The Woman in American History*. Menlo Park, CA: Addison-Wesley, 1971.

Mann, Barbara Alice. *George Washington's War on Native America*. Westport, CT: Praeger, 2005.

———. *Iroquoian Women: The Gantowisas*. New York: Peter Lang, 2000.

———. *Land of the Three Miamis: A Traditional Narrative of the Iroquois*. Toledo, OH: University of Toledo Urban Affairs Center Press, 2006.

———. *Native Americans, Archaeologists, and the Mounds*. New York: Peter Lang, 2003.

Melmer, David. "Women Join Together in South Dakota." *Indian Country Today* 9 Feb. 2007. 23 Oct 2007 <*http://www.indiancountrytoday.com/content/cfm?id=1096414479*>.

———. "Women Set Up Network to Support Their Issues." *Indian Country Today* 5 Feb. 2007. 23 Oct 2007 <*http://www.indiancountrytoday.com/cfm?id=1096414441*>.

Norrell, Brenda. "Ending Violence against Women Made a Priority." *Indian Country Today* 23 November 2005, B1.

———. "Indigenous Women Filmmakers Network." *Indian Country Today* 28 July 2004, D1.

Sherman, Julia A. and Evelyn Torton Beck. *The Prism of Sex: Essays in the Sociology of Knowledge.* Madison: University of Wisconsin Press, 1979.